Work, Leisure and the Environment

For Veronica, Chloe, Thomas and Nicola

Work, Leisure and the Environment

The Vicious Circle of Overwork and
Over Consumption

Tim Robinson

School of Economics and Finance, Queensland University of Technology

Edward Elgar
Cheltenham, UK · Northhampton, MA, USA

Published by
Edward Elgar Publishing Limited
Glensanda House
Montpellier Parade
Cheltenham
Glos GL50 1UA
UK

Edward Elgar Publishing, Inc.
William Pratt House
9 Dewey Court
Northampton
Massachusetts 01060
USA

A catalogue record for this book
is available from the British Library

Library of Congress Cataloguing in Publication Data
Robinson, T. J. C. (Tim J. C.), 1945–
  Work, leisure, and the environment : the vicious circle of overwork and
over consumption / Tim Robinson.
      p. cm.
  Includes bibliographical references and index.
  1. Consumption (Economics)—Environmental aspects—United States. 2.
Hours of labor—Social aspects—United States. 3. Leisure—Social
aspects—United States. 4. Work—Social aspects—United States. 5.
United States—Economic policy. I. Title. II. Title: Overwork and over
consumption.
  HC110.C6R63 2006
  306.3'60973—dc22

                                        2006021064

ISBN-13: 978 1 84720 103 4
ISBN-10: 1 84720 103 2

Contents

Figures

Abbreviations

ACTU	Australian Council of Trade Unions
EAI	environmentally adjusted income
FISH	Fordham Index of Social Health
GDP	gross domestic product
GPI	Genuine Progress Indicator
IPAT	impact population affluence technology
ISEW	Index of Sustainable Economic Welfare
IWB	Index of Well-being
OECD	Organisation for Economic Co-operation and Development
QOL	quality of life
SUV	sport utility vehicle

Acknowledgements

This work has had a long gestation period during the course of which I have been assisted in many ways by many people. First, and most importantly, thanks go to my wife and three children who, by brightening my days, have made this task so much easier. Second, I would like to thank the individuals who have read the manuscript and made so many worthwhile comments and suggestions; they include James K. Boyce, Tony Harland, Veronica Horgan, Ted Kolsen, Oskar Kurer, Allan Layton and Zoe McHugh. Thanks also to those who helped in other ways. They include James Bondio, Stan Hurn and Maria Robinson as well as two anonymous reviewers. Of course, none of this would have been possible without the enthusiasm of people at Edward Elgar including Edward himself, Felicity Plester and Suzanne Mursell. Finally, thanks to the School of Economics and Finance at Queensland University of Technology and my colleagues there who have been supportive at all times.

By their very nature adventurous pursuits, such as the one undertaken in the writing of this book, are accompanied by risk. Needless to say, any costs associated with that risk are to be borne by the author.

Preface

This book is about a fundamental flaw in contemporary market economies that causes individuals to voluntarily work and consume too much while enjoying too little leisure. In working and consuming too much they are placing unreasonable and unsustainable demands on the environment. Furthermore, as the arguments in this book explain, unless the fundamental flaw is acknowledged and acted upon, humankind faces ever increasing environmental disamenity. This is because the characteristics of the fundamental flaw mean that the current problems of overwork and consequent environmental degradation reinforce each other leading us further and further away from the optimum. Over time, the extent to which work is excessive in relation to leisure grows continually along with the extent of environmental degradation. This is the outcome of the vicious circle of overwork and over consumption.

My interest in the relationship between work, leisure and the environment was prompted by a number of factors. First, in my own personal life I seem to have been observing more and more people (and families) who are increasingly busy but who are seemingly not gaining increases in their well-being that are commensurate with that increased busyness. Second, the burgeoning literature dealing with issues relating to work-life balance suggests that the developed world is more interested in these issues today than at any time in the past half of a century. Whether one looks in academic journals, business or lifestyle magazines, or television programmes and books, one finds a growing volume of material dealing with problems associated with excessive work effort and inadequate leisure. Third, and finally, the explanations in the literature of the reasons for these work-related problems seemed to me to be diverse, unconvincing and without rigour. As an economist I wondered whether there was, nonetheless, a sound economic reason for them. After all it is a basic tenet of economic theory that problems such as these can only occur in the market economies of democratic nations if they display some inherent flaw. It is the task of this work to help explain that there is such a flaw and give reasons for it.

Although this book is written by an economist, it is, for a number of reasons, written primarily for non-economists. The first and most important reason that it is written for non-economists relates to the fact that most of the growing literature dealing with overwork, consumerism and work-life balance is written by non-economists for non-economist readers who are seeking explanations for these problems. Rather than write what, from the lay person's perspective, would be seen as an esoteric piece of theoretical and applied economics, this book is an attempt to place the economic explanation for overwork into the more general literature by expressing economic arguments in an accessible form. The fundamental explanation for overwork that is put forward in this book is one that is very different from other explanations of this phenomenon; it deserves to be read by as wide an audience as possible.

The second reason that this book is written primarily for non-economists is that the explanation for overwork which is put forward here is intimately connected with environmental degradation. Only if this explanation is expressed in an accessible way can it become a part of the wider literature dealing with explanations for our overwhelming environmental problems.

A third reason for targeting this book at non-economists relates to the changing philosophical stance that contributions to mainstream economics have displayed in recent times. Whereas, in the first three quarters of the 20th century, economists gave increasing emphasis to the usefulness of economics in dealing with those many instances where laissez-faire was found wanting, in the past three decades these shortcomings have been de-emphasized in favour of a championing of the benefits of free market economies. The current philosophical stance of many economists is one which prevents them from acknowledging that contemporary economies may display characteristics that prevent the maximizing of the well-being of society. This being the case, there is a risk that if this book were written for economists alone, its message would fall on too many deaf ears. This having been said, it should be emphasized that there are many economists doing good work in areas that are concerned with the shortcomings of markets and market economies – shortcomings that economists often describe as market failures. I hope that they will read this book and forgive me for what, to them, will sometimes appear to be rather circuitous ways of explaining my thesis.

Finally, like many of my thoughtful economist colleagues, I am aware of the shortcomings and limitations of contemporary economic theory; nonetheless, as the pages that follow will, I hope, show, this theory constitutes a very powerful tool that can, in combination with deliberative thought processes, help explain a phenomenon such as overwork in a more rigorous way than has been hitherto provided.

Tim Robinson
School of Economics and Finance and Institute for Sustainable Resources
Queensland University of Technology

1. Economic Approaches to the Environment

Almost without exception, the message we have heard, a message of deep concern, has been the same: the American Dream just doesn't seem to be coming true any more. Life at the dawn of the millennium isn't what it should be. It seems that our economic and technical progress has not succeeded in bringing about the good society. A higher standard of living has somehow failed to result in a better quality of life.[1]

Andres Duany et al

In spite of claims that humankind has never before reached such a high standard of living as is experienced today, there seems to be a generalized dissatisfaction with our lot. In the words of Professor of Social Epidemiology, Richard Wilkinson: 'The contrast between the material success and social failure of modern societies is a profound paradox, and we have little understanding of the causal processes responsible for it.'[2] Indeed, there has been no time in recent history when such a large range of interrelated factors – including family breakdown, loss of community, stress, crime, environmental degradation and inadequate leisure time – has provided evidence of such a malaise. Furthermore, the search for solutions to today's problems is clouded by the question of whether these interrelated factors should be seen as causes of this malaise or merely evidence of it.

Every student of economics learns that economic theory can be used to demonstrate that a system of competitive capitalism maximizes the well-being of the community. For some reason, however, the current malaise in the capitalist system indicates that it is failing to deliver. Is this because there is something inherently wrong with capitalism as critics from the left assert, or is the problem that the capitalist system does not operate in the way that the theory says it does? Is the problem, to paraphrase the words of John Maynard Keynes, that the characteristics of the special case assumed by the theory happen not to be those of the economic society in which we actually live?[3]

If this is the correct explanation, and if the cause of this disjuncture between the way in which the economy actually operates and the way in which the theory says it operates can be detected, then it would be possible to take steps to correct the situation.

This book is about a fundamental flaw in the capitalist system that causes us to unknowingly reduce our well-being by working and consuming too much. The basic argument that will be developed here is that, of their own free will, individuals choose to destroy work-life balance by working longer hours than are consistent with maximization of their own well-being. They do this because a fundamental flaw in the system prevents them from correctly assessing the benefits they derive from their work effort. Because they overestimate the benefits of their work effort, they choose to work longer hours than they should.

In order to explain how this flaw contributes to the malaise in contemporary society, this book concentrates on two key manifestations of this malaise: 1) environmental degradation, and 2) inadequate leisure. It will demonstrate that these two phenomena are closely interrelated. The excessive work effort of most individuals will be shown to be both a result of, and a significant cause of, contemporary environmental degradation. The question of whether many of the other factors cited in the first paragraph of this chapter as evidence of a widespread malaise in contemporary society are also related to a deficit of leisure is left for readers to ponder and researchers to pursue.[4]

In recent decades a heightened understanding of the extent to which economic activity degrades the environment has led to an ever increasing number of ad hoc policies designed to correct the situation. But is this ad hoc approach appropriate to the task? In the next section this piecemeal approach and its shortcomings are compared with the benefits of a more holistic approach – an approach that might have as its centrepiece a reduction in work hours, consumption and ensuing environmental degradation.

THE NEED FOR A HOLISTIC APPROACH

The history of environmental policy is the history of a series of ad hoc attempts to solve whatever is perceived to be the most pressing problem of the time. At the height of the oil crises of the 1970s we were assailed by the prophets of doom who told us that we should look forward to a future of ever increasing energy prices. Among the sillier suggestions of the time was that we should develop sailing ships to transport freight on the high seas. Remember the economy gauges that were once found in the instrument clusters of many automobiles? They were a short-lived feature that told us whether our driving style was energy efficient. Until recently, in the wider community, oil and, more generally, energy availability was perceived to be one of the least of our environmental problems. The penchant for large, gas-guzzling SUVs and for energy-intensive heating and air-conditioning systems in our homes was testimony to this. All this changed, however, with the re-emergence of high oil prices in 2005. The complacency that characterized the closing decades of the 20th century has been replaced with a renewed fear of an energy crisis. All of a sudden small motor vehicles and home insulation have a new-found popularity.

In an international context, global warming associated with climate change is currently perceived to be society's number one problem, with vast resources and mammoth talk fests being devoted to policy solutions. What about the hole in the ozone layer? Although it seems to have taken a back seat in recent times, it may well emerge as a serious problem in the future. At the national and local levels, governments are endeavouring to tackle problems of motor vehicle pollution, urban sprawl, threats to biodiversity, loss of wilderness areas and open space, dwindling water resources, salination and waste disposal. Moreover, we know not what the future may bring by way of unexpected unpleasant consequences of our present activities. Past activities such as the widespread use of lead, asbestos, DDT and CFCs, that seemed benign at the time, have had devastating environmental effects.[5]

The ad hoc nature of our approach to the environment means that our attention, and that of politicians and policy-makers, is grabbed by whatever environmental problem is prominent at the time. As historian, ecologist and environmentalist Jared Diamond has put it, the single most important environmental/population problem facing the world today is 'our misguided focus on identifying the single most important problem'![6] Too little emphasis is given to the far more important question of the development of an overall policy thrust aimed at solving our environmental problems once and for all – or, at least, aimed at achieving a steady improvement of our level of environmental amenity. This ad hoc approach has even infected the OECD which, in its *Work Programme on Sustainable Consumption and Production*, emphasizes that 'the sustainable consumption and production debate is not de facto an agenda for reducing consumption in general...[A]ction to promote sustainability must be based on a case-by-case analysis of potential constraints to consumption and production of any particular good, service or natural resource'.[7] The problem with the OECD's preferred case-by-case approach is, as Ropke points out, that 'the environmental benefits of a change in consumption practices in one area can easily be counterbalanced by increased consumption in other areas, if growth is not limited.'[8] Thus, for example, a policy of reducing consumption of fish so as to ensure the long-term future of ocean fisheries might result in an increase in environmentally damaging overgrazing as the population of ruminants increases.

In a more recent document, the OECD unwittingly acknowledges that the overall level of consumption itself can be the villain of the piece:

> In areas such as household energy use, travel and waste generation, material and energy efficiency gains have been outweighed by the volume of goods and services that are consumed and discarded.[9]

Echoing the OECD's preferred case-by-case approach, the Clinton Administration's Population and Consumption Task Force addressed environmental problems associated with consumption by suggesting a wide array of ad hoc policies ranging from public education programmes and harnessing religious commitment through to eco-labelling and the introduction of volume-based garbage fees. The Task Force did no more than pay lip service to the holistic solution involving reduced consumption resulting from reduced work hours, although they quoted the '...[n]early 70 per cent of Americans who would like to "slow down and live a more relaxed life".'[10]

It is the contention of this book that a holistic approach to improvement of the environment is required in both national and international arenas. Slowly, in the area of human health we are seeing the ad hoc curative approaches of the past being complemented by holistic preventative policies designed to ensure a healthy lifestyle. Our approach to the environment should be no different; rather than merely dealing with problems in a piecemeal fashion when they rear their ugly heads, we should be following a path that minimizes their incidence in the first place. To be sure, this holistic approach will need to be complemented by ad hoc policies that tackle the worst of our day-to-day environmental excesses. Nonetheless, as is the case with health policy, prevention is often better than cure. But how best can such a holistic approach be implemented?

Implementing a Holistic Approach

Many environmentalists have suggested that a holistic approach involving a sea-change in human values wrought by education, religion or propaganda is what is required – a movement towards a simpler, more austere lifestyle founded upon a philosophical commitment to care for nature. Unfortunately, in liberal democracies – say nothing of authoritarian regimes – these approaches have been manifestly unsuccessful. At the national level, the onset of a mild recession is all that is required to guarantee a call from politicians and policy-makers for the pursuit of economic growth at all costs – including the relaxation of environmental policies eagerly introduced in more prosperous times. At the individual level, it appears that self-interest is guaranteed to override concern for the environment whenever there is a clash between the two. Remember the baby-boomers of the 1960s who tuned in, turned on, and dropped out to a simpler lifestyle in communes at the beach or in the woods? Where are they now? All but a few gave up the simple alternative. Today they are part of the richest generation in living memory – a generation that degrades the environment in a way that would seem unimaginable to their forebears. In the name of a simpler, cleaner lifestyle we continually hear calls for more use of solar and wind power to limit fossil fuel usage and pollution. My parents used both of these forms of power to dry the clothes on the washing line. Today's parents – environmentally aware though they may be – are more inclined to use the ubiquitous clothes drier driven by fossil fuel power.

But are today's parents as environmentally aware as they seem? Almost 30 years ago, professor of human ecology and author of *The Tragedy of the Commons*, Garrett Hardin questioned humankind's ecological literacy:

> [W]hat proportion of the earth's population understands the immensely destructive power of man's everyday actions? I would be surprised if it is as great as one in a thousand. We have a long way to go before this knowledge sufficiently influences policy. We are shocked at a country that is 90 per cent illiterate. Our rate of ecological literacy, which is at least as high, poses an even greater threat to the interests of posterity.[11]

Judging by the behaviour of the typical citizen, it would be surprising if much has changed since these words were written – even in the world's richest countries.

Political and environmental scientist Michael Maniates notes the dissonance in our everyday approaches to environmental issues:

> As individual consumers and recyclers we are supplied with ample and easy means of 'doing our bit' – green consumerism and militant recycling becomes the order of the day. The result, though, is often dissonant and sometimes bizarre: consumers wearing 'save the earth' T-shirts, for example, speak passionately against recent rises in gasoline prices when approached by television news crews; shoppers drive all over town in their gasoline-guzzling SUVs in search of organic lettuce or shade-grown coffee; and diligent recyclers expend far more fossil-fuel energy on the hot water spent to meticulously clean a tin can than is saved by its recycling.[12]

Even among environment advocates themselves we continually see examples of such dissonance. Recently, the first member of the Greens party ever elected to the lower house in Australia's national parliament was exposed as intending to use a gas-guzzling turbo-charged motor car as his official form of transport.[13] At how many social gatherings have you witnessed idle chatter about environmental problems and the need for action, followed by the intake of too much food and drink by people who then drive away in cars too big and powerful for their needs to distant homes with a bathroom for every bedroom? It seems that the individualistic, self-interested foundations of contemporary society are too strong to allow an environment-regarding philosophy to take root.[14] With the demise of communism and the surge in support for free market solutions, this tendency appears to have become even more evident in recent times. But does this love affair with the market mean that a long-term solution to our environmental problems is unattainable?

Given that the basic thrust of free market economies appears to be the pursuit of ever greater levels of material welfare, it might seem that there is no possible way in which an economic approach could provide the solution;

for, in essence, the solution lies in decreasing the level of economic activity and the environmental degradation that goes with it. In other words, if it is not possible (or desirable) to change the philosophical roots that underlie liberal democracies, does this mean that there is no way in which a holistic approach to the environment can be fostered that is consistent with the tenets of competitive capitalism? This book shows that there is such a way. Rather than working against market outcomes in order to improve the environment, this way actually improves market outcomes by countering the effects of the fundamental flaw in the market economy that causes us to make unsustainable demands on the environment by working too much and consuming too much. Furthermore, it will be shown that in addition to making unsustainable demands on the environment, the current overemphasis on work and consumption actually leads to a lower level of human happiness than could otherwise be achieved.

Lest it be thought that the assertion that the economy is characterized by a fundamental flaw means that the liberal economic tradition is itself flawed, it should be made clear that this book is based on the premise that this is not so. Indeed the underlying disciplinary foundation of this book is the mainstream economic model that has been developed and progressively refined over the more than 200 years since it was created at the hands of Adam Smith. The fundamental flaw that characterizes the economy is, as we shall see, a flaw that can be eliminated or, at least, accounted for, in a way that increases economic welfare in the market economy. Furthermore, it is the mainstream economic model that provides the tools that enable us to detect and deal with this flaw

WHY THE LIBERAL ECONOMIC TRADITION?

The liberal economic tradition is the term that will be used here to describe advocacy of an economic system that is characterized by democracy, individual liberty, private property rights and competition between economic agents. That is, an economic system in which markets are the predominant means of determining what types of goods and services will be produced, what quantities of these goods and services will be produced, and how income and wealth will be distributed. The liberal economic tradition does not, and never has, eschewed the mixed economy in which there is a role for the state in taxing, spending and making laws consistent with the will of the people. In this respect enlightened economists are unlike Miss Cummins, the school principal from the William story 'Guy Fawkes – with Variations', who, after meeting a brusque William dressed as her cousin's daughter, could not 'remember feeling so shaken since the time a visiting lecturer had deliberately introduced Socialism into a lecture on Economics.'[15] To be sure, some advocates argue for a minimalist role for the state; nonetheless, most economists acknowledge that state intervention in some areas of economic activity may provide better outcomes than pure laissez-faire. As an example of support for this position, consider the following quote from economist and Nobel Prize winner Robert Solow.

> There are many questions on which the [individualist criterion] does not speak at all and it *must* [original emphasis] be supplemented by sharper value judgements that each society must make in its own characteristic way. For example, the strict individualist criterion does not imply that it would have been a good idea for the English government to have relieved starvation in Ireland during the potato famine. It was, however, a fallacy for the English to believe, as some of them did, that the criterion did imply that it would have been a bad thing. It is simply a separate decision.[16]

A huge body of economic literature has been developed within the liberal economic tradition. Much of it is concerned with ways in which government can improve the operation of the economy by actions such as: redefining and reassigning property rights; using taxing and spending powers to redistribute income and to discourage or encourage particular activities; and, finally, framing macroeconomic policies that attempt to promote full employment, low inflation and economic growth. Nonetheless, the underlying tenet of the liberal economic tradition is that individuals are the best judges of their own welfare and should, accordingly, be given a great deal of freedom to pursue their own happiness in the ways that they see fit. Consistent with the principles of liberalism, they should do so in a way that guarantees the liberty of their fellow human beings.

Advocates of laissez-faire capitalism are often accused of promoting unenlightened self-interest – what is sometimes described as greed. Some of them do. The liberal economic tradition does not. It is concerned to promote the efficient working of free market economies subject to conformity to an underlying set of ethical or moral principles – a set of principles that are not to be traded for increased material welfare. As Adam Smith pointed out over two centuries ago, the gaining of economic advantage by nonconformity to these principles does not promote the economic welfare of the community.[17] Nonetheless, management guru, Charles Handy, is probably right when he says that as a community,

> [w]e misinterpreted Adam Smith's ideas to mean that if we each looked after our own interests, some 'invisible hand' would mysteriously arrange things so that it all worked out for the best for all. We therefore promulgated the rights of the individual and freedom of choice for all. But without the accompanying requirements of self-restraint; without thought for one's neighbour, and one's grandchildren such freedom becomes licence and then mere selfishness. Adam Smith, who was professor of moral philosophy, not of economics, built his theories on the basis of a moral community. Before he wrote *A Theory of the Wealth of Nations* he had written his definitive work – *A Theory of Moral Sentiments* –

arguing that a stable society was based on 'sympathy', a moral duty to have regard for your fellow human beings. The market is a mechanism for sorting the efficient from the inefficient, it is not a substitute for responsibility.[18]

So much for the liberal economic tradition; but why use its methodology as a basis for analysing the relationships between work, leisure and the environment?

THE NATURE OF ECONOMICS

Economics prides itself on being the most exacting of the social sciences – akin in its methodology to, say, physics. This claim stems from the use of a rigorous theoretical superstructure built on a foundation comprised of a set of simple and immutable assumptions about the nature of human beings and their fundamental motivations. The essence of these simple assumptions is that individuals attempt to determine the appropriate trade-off between pleasurable activities (for example, consumption and leisure) and the unpleasurable activities (for example, work) that make these pleasurable activities possible. Quoting the 19th-century liberal economist John Stuart Mill, his successor, celebrated English economist Alfred Marshall, put it this way.

> It is true that the forces with which economics deals have one advantage for deductive treatment in the fact that their method of combination is, as Mill observed, that of mechanics rather than of chemistry. That is to say, when we know the action of two economic forces separately – as for instance the influences which an increase in the rate of wages and a diminution in the difficulty of the work in a trade will severally exert on the supply of labour in it – we can predict fairly well their conjoint action, without waiting for specific experience of it.[19]

The rigour of the economics discipline has also been aided by the discovery of a number of economic laws akin to those of the physical sciences.

The best known of the early exponents of this rigorous analytical approach in economics was the early 19th-century English economist David Ricardo. His successors had refined his pioneering work to such an extent that by the close of the 19th century the fundamental methodology that underpins all mainstream economic analysis today had been developed. This economic paradigm has shown great resilience over the past century.

At the heart of this economic paradigm is the assumption that we are rational beings set upon maximizing our well-being in the context of our own set of personal preferences. This assumption does not mean that concern for groups of friends and colleagues or for our families is not able to be dealt with by the basic economic model. Indeed, much economic analysis is concerned with the behaviour of groups – with the family or household often being substituted for the individual as the basic unit in economic models. In this book, the traditional emphasis upon decisions made by the individual will be maintained; although it is acknowledged that in many, if not most, instances, those decisions will be made in the context of the interests of the family or household unit to which the individual belongs.

The analysis that follows in this book concentrates on the relationship between two key contributors to our happiness — leisure time and the quality of the environment. These contributors to our happiness have each been subject to intense scrutiny by many individuals including academics from a wide range of disciplines, journalists, policy-makers, and populist agitators and authors. So why is it that we are going to look beyond the work of these individuals to see what an analysis based on the liberal economic tradition can reveal?

WHY EMPLOY THE ECONOMIC PARADIGM?

The fundamental reason for using the economic paradigm to analyse the relationship between leisure and the environment is found in the disinterested nature of its methodology. On the basis of the fundamental assumptions of the economic model, it is possible to use this methodology to determine whether individuals in the economy are currently behaving in such a way as to maximize their well-being. In the pages that follow, we are going to discover that, because of a fundamental flaw in the system, individuals do not, in fact, behave in such a way as to maximize their well-being. They work too much, consume too much and have too little leisure. Once we have established this, we can then use the economic model to examine policy proposals that will help correct the situation.

Those readers familiar with the literature dealing with the environment and with the issues of mass consumption and leisure will know that there seem to be as many prognoses and prescriptions as there are authors writing on these subjects. Much of the literature is highly subjective, alarmist and concerned with policy solutions that seem fanciful to ordinary citizens. By contrast, use of the liberal economic approach enables us to determine what the nature of the problem is, and possible solutions to it, in a way that resonates with the day-to-day behaviour of typical citizens who want the economic system to deliver quality of life without the need for conformity to an obscure set of philosophical beliefs or social mores.

The power of the economic paradigm in analysing work-related environmental issues can be illustrated by analysing the claim that not only will improved environmental outcomes result from a reduction in work hours but also these reduced work hours need not be accompanied by a reduction in workers' pay. The most commonly cited argument for no reduction in workers' pay involves the idea that increased leisure raises the amount of capital per worker as well as refreshing workers in such a way as to result in no decrease in output.[20] A little reflection reveals that if there is no decrease in output there will be little or no change in the level of environmental damage. In other words, the economic model tells us that an attempt to protect the environment by having workers work fewer hours, but produce as much output as ever, is doomed to fail. Furthermore, and more importantly, the economic model tells us that there is no such thing as a free lunch – all other factors remaining unchanged, a reduction of work hours from their current level must be accompanied by a decrease in output. What the economic model does not tell us, however, is that such a reduction in work hours accompanied by a fall in output and consumption will not necessarily reduce our well-being. Later we will use economic theory to demonstrate that workers will raise their well-being by working shorter hours, even though they will receive lower work-related incomes as a consequence.

Like many other concerns, the issue of the relationship between leisure and the environment is one in which deep differences of opinion are displayed. On the one hand, among left-leaning politicians, environmentalists, unionists, sociologists and pop psychologists there are likely to be many strong advocates of increased leisure and reduced environmental degradation. On the other hand, among business leaders, conservative politicians and the rural community there are likely to be many advocates of the work ethic who see the environmental degradation as posing few problems.

Who is right? A reading of contributions to the debate from both sides leaves us uncertain as to whom to believe. Each side seems to be as adamant as the other in its claim to supremacy. Much of the literature appears to preach to the converted – and the converted often seek out this literature in order to confirm their own beliefs.

The economist's approach is different. The objective is to marshal the available information and analyse it using the tried and true methodology, without recourse to the subjective beliefs or values of the author. Just as an engineer can determine why a piece of machinery is performing poorly and suggest a solution, so the economist can analyse the state of the economy – or sectors of it – and suggest policy solutions. By and large, it does not matter whether the engineer is conservative or progressive, God-fearing or atheist; the diagnosis and the proposed solution will, if the engineer is a good engineer, be much the same. The same can be said of good economists.[21]

In order to progress the argument, the role that economists can play in analysing the two key aspects of contemporary society that are the subject of this book – leisure and the environment – is examined.

ENVIRONMENT, LEISURE AND THE ROLE OF ECONOMICS

In relation to solutions to our environmental problems, the first thing to be said is that the expertise of environmentalists and environmental scientists should be directed primarily at measuring the extent of environmental damage that has occurred or may occur, and then suggesting the nature of remedial actions that could be implemented. By contrast, the economist's expertise lies in determining the costs of environmental damage (based on the environmental scientist's estimate of the physical and other changes that are wrought), the costs of remedial action that might be taken (again based on the scientist's estimates of what might be done) and the benefits to be gained from the taking of remedial action. Although the literature is replete with dire warnings from environmentalists and environmental scientists as to the costs to humanity of specific instances of current or potential environmental damage, it is, in fact, the economist who is trained to use the facts that the scientists generate to determine the policy responses that maximizes well-being. The work of environmentalists and environmental scientists is crucial to a determination of appropriate policy responses; but the input of economists should be an important element in the process.[22]

Looking at leisure, we find that there is a vast literature dealing with either leisure itself or, more often, with the consumption that is enabled by the decision to engage in work by sacrificing leisure. Much of this is populist literature critical of the central role that consumerism plays in contemporary society. This literature variously targets the advertising industry, the promotion of brand names, the capitalist system itself or the frailty of humans who are deemed incapable of controlling their own patterns of work and consumption.[23] Nonetheless, there are branches of this literature, particularly those contributed by sociologists and psychologists, that are scientific in their nature and which contribute greatly to our understanding of the attitudes of human beings to leisure and consumption. From time to time in this book we will have cause to refer to this literature which has important contributions to make to our understanding of human behaviour. It is, however, not central to our analysis. This is because the economic approach we are going to use here is less concerned with the underlying basis of people's behaviour, and more concerned with the ways in which this behaviour is manifested through what economists describe as revealed preferences. Labour economist Bruce Kaufman points to the success of the conventional economic approach in spite of the limitations of its 'unrealistic representation of the nature of human beings'. Pointing out that, over the years, numerous critics have had fun satirizing this unrealistic representation with the apparent objective of discrediting mainstream economics as a discipline, he argues that not only is this strategy unscientific but that it has manifestly failed. Quoting Baron and Hannon he says that the mainstream economist's rational choice model 'continues to dominate economics and is rapidly gaining ground in sociology, political science, and other social science disciplines.'[24]

The economic approach to the relationship between leisure and consumption that is developed here sees individuals making decisions about foregoing leisure so that they can engage in unpleasant work that provides the wherewithal to undertake consumption.

A NOTE ON CONCEPTS AND TERMINOLOGY

As noted in the Preface, this book is written primarily for the non-economist. It endeavours to use non-technical language wherever possible. In many cases familiar everyday terms are substituted for the technical jargon of the economist. However, where it is best to use that jargon, the meaning of the terms employed is made clear.

It is important to point out at this stage that whenever economists use the term cost they mean sacrifices. Contrary to popular belief, economists are not concerned only with monetary expenditure. Although economists are sometimes tagged as cynics who, in Oscar Wilde's words, know the price of everything and the value of nothing, the reality is that good economists know the prices of some things and the values of many more.

There are many costs incurred by individuals, groups and society that are not expressed on a day-to-day basis in dollar terms. Because the term cost is a synonym for sacrifice, a raft of non-traded sacrifices are described as involving costs. Some of the more important sacrifices that we describe as costs here include the sacrifice of a clean environment that accompanies pollution, the sacrifice of leisure that occurs when we work, the sacrifice of time and other resources that is brought about by congestion, and the sacrifice of alternative uses of leisure time that occurs when we engage in a particular leisure activity. To these non-monetary sacrifices we can add the costs of monetary purchases that involve the sacrifice of purchasing power.

Some of my economist colleagues will be shocked by the rough-and-ready calculations employed in this book. Without accusing them of an unrealistic approach to the potential rigour of their discipline, it is worth while pointing out that economic research itself is as much subject to the principles of optimization as are the subjects of that research. Interpreting Herbert Simon in their analysis of rules of thumb, Baumol and Quandt aver that business decision-makers do not usually attempt to find the optimum solutions '...precisely because they recognize the limited accuracy of their information and excessive costs of persnickety calculation, and that, instead, they are well satisfied with viable solutions to their problems.'[25] This book presents a first approximation to a viable solution to the question of why work hours are excessive. Further research may have the potential to greatly refine this solution.

WHAT THIS BOOK IS NOT ABOUT

This book investigates the costs to the community of excessive hours of paid work; that is, work carried out in the workplace as opposed to volunteer work or work in the home. As we shall see in the next chapter, a fundamental flaw in the economic system causes us to work excessive hours of paid work because we are prevented from accurately determining the amount of this work that maximizes our well-being. In some recent studies of work it has been argued that it is necessary to include both paid work and unpaid work to determine the extent to which our overall hours of work are excessive.[26] An understanding of the economics of the motivation to work, which is discussed in the following chapters, will be used to explain that the potential for unpaid work hours to be excessive is far less than in the case of paid work. Furthermore, as we shall see later, unpaid work such as volunteering or cooking, cleaning and child-minding undertaken in the home, is likely to be more environmentally benign than work undertaken in the workplace.

In his quirky novel *The Scheme for Full Employment*, Magnus Mills describes a state-funded enterprise that creates full-time work for its employees but which produces no useful output. In an exchange between two of the novel's characters who are employees of the scheme, the issue of employees being allowed to finish early each day is discussed. One of the characters observes that there seems to be a contradiction between a scheme for full employment and the oft fulfilled desire of the employees to skive off early and thus be employed for fewer hours. His fellow employee replies that 'the point is ... there's a difference between full employment and being fully employed.' He goes on: '[t]rue, there is a lot of spare capacity in The Scheme, but it's better for people to be paid to do very little than have no job at all, isn't it?'[27] As political scientist and commentator, Francis Fukuyama, implies in his discussions of the origins of work in *The End of History and the Last Man*, economists are unlikely to agree with the sentiment expressed in this last statement even though they may understand that dignity, self-esteem and companionship accompany work.[28] From the economist's perspective, work typically involves displeasure while leisure generates pleasure. The sacrifice of leisure in order to be employed to do very little, as is the case in the scheme for full employment, makes little economic sense.

It is argued in much of the literature dealing with the need for reduced hours of work that fewer hours of paid work per employee would reduce unemployment by increasing employment opportunities for the unemployed.[29] Although we shall touch briefly upon this idea of sharing the work by reducing hours for those already employed, it is not an important part of the argument presented here. The basic assumption employed here is that with the assistance of sound national economic policies, full employment can normally be achieved in mixed economies regardless of the number of hours worked by employees. Support for this position can be found in the achievement of full employment in different countries regardless of the number of hours typically worked by their employees. Support is also found indirectly in the maintenance of full employment over the course of recent history in spite of marked increases in the participation rate of women. The use of this full employment assumption is not meant to constitute an apologia for the capitalist system. So devastating are the effects of unemployment that politicians and policy-makers in mixed economies must be ever mindful of their responsibility to eliminate it.[30]

There are many ills that reduce the well-being of individuals in contemporary society. They include crime, family breakdown, addiction to recreational drugs, loss of community, environmental degradation and congestion. This book emphasizes those ills that are directly related to the level of national output per capita. These are the ills that will be lessened by shorter work hours and a concomitant decrease in output. Although many of the ills cited here – including crime, family breakdown and loss of community – are often linked to long work hours, there is no hard evidence of a causal relationship.[31] On the other hand, there is strong evidence that environmental degradation and congestion are directly related to the per capita level of economic activity. Later, in Chapter 6, we shall see that there is incontrovertible evidence that nations with high levels of output per capita are responsible for high levels of environmental degradation per capita. Every increase in output per capita also has the potential to increase congestion. Whether it be more and bigger automobiles on our roads, larger houses and building lots that contribute to urban sprawl, or increasingly crowded beaches, each of these developments is exacerbated by higher levels of output per capita.[32] Environmental degradation and congestion are, of course, inextricably linked. For example, congestion on our roads increases air pollution which can be simply described as the *congestion* of clean air by pollutants. Although we shall frequently consider environmental degradation and congestion as separate phenomena, we do so in the knowledge that they are inextricably intertwined.

In the next chapter we look at how the level of work effort is determined in capitalist economies, and how a fundamental flaw in the economic system causes individuals to mistakenly allocate too much of their time to work and too little to leisure.

The last word is given to 19th-century wit, Oscar Wilde, whose views on economics (or political economy as it was more often described then) suggest that the problem of an economy that fails to deliver what the people want is nothing new.

I am going to write a Political Economy in my heavier moments. The first law I lay down is 'Wherever there exists a demand, there is no supply.' This is the only law that explains the extraordinary contrast between the soul of man, and man's surroundings. Civilizations continue because people hate them. A modern city is the exact opposite of what everyone wants. Nineteenth-century dress is the result of our horror of the style. The tall hat will last as long as the people dislike it.[33]

NOTES

1   Duany, A., Plater-Zyberk, E. and Speck, S. (2000), *Suburban Nation,* New York: North Point Press, p. xii.
2   Wilkinson Richard G. (2005), *The Impact of Inequality*, New York: The Free Press, p.5. I am indebted to Elizabeth Faldt who referred me to Wilkinson's work.
3   Keynes, J.M. (1936), *The General Theory of Employment Interest and Money*, London: Macmillan, p. 3.
4   Richard Douthwaite has no doubt that they do. See Douthwaite, R. (1999), *The Growth Illusion*, Gabriola Island: New Society Publishers. Also see Madeleine Bunting's argument that there is a crisis in human sustainability caused by the decline in human interdependence associated with over work. Bunting, Madeleine (2004), *Willing Slaves*, London: HarperCollins, p. 178.
5   See Princen, T. (2002), 'Distancing: Consumption and the Severing of Feedback', Chap. 5 in Princen, T., Maniates, M. and Conca, K. (2002), *Confronting Consumption*, Cambridge, MA: MIT Press, p. 109.
6   See Diamond, J. (2005), *Collapse*, Camberwell: Allen Lane, p. 498.
7   Ropke, I. (1999), 'The dynamics of willingness to consume', *Ecological Economics*, **28** (3), p. 401.
8   Ibid.
9   OECD (2002), 'Towards Sustainable Household Consumption? trends and policies in OECD countries', Paris: OECD, p. 89.
10   Population and Consumption Task Force, *Report*, 'Chapter 2: Consumption', p.15 at http://clinton2.nara.gov/PCSD/Publications/TF_Reports/pop-toc.htm, accessed 2 July 2004.
11   Hardin, Garrett (1977), *The Limits of Altruism*, Bloomington: Indiana University Press, p. 34.
12   Maniates, M. (2002), 'Individualization: Plant a Tree, Buy a Bike, Save the World?', Chap. 3 in Princen, T., Maniates, M. and Conca, K., *Confronting Consumption*, Cambridge MA: MIT Press, p. 55.
13   Maguire, Tory (2002), 'Racing Green - New MP asks for a gas guzzler that drinks 12 litres per 100km', *The Sydney Daily Telegraph*, 28 December, p. 5.
14   I am indebted to an anonymous reviewer who pointed me in the direction of Tim Jackson and Laurie Michaelis's report to the Sustainable Development Commission in which they make the point that 'evolutionary psychology points to the limitations of appealing to the "better nature" of consumers.' They go on to argue that '[e]xhortations to individual restraint are likely to be meet (sic) with limited success, particularly where social conditions militate against altruistic behaviour.' Jackson, Tim and Michaelis, Laurie (2003), 'Policies for Sustainable Consumption', at http://www.sd-commission.org.uk/publications/downloads/030917%20Policies%20for%sustainable%20consumption%20_SD C%20report_.pdf, accessed 28 April 2006.
15   Crompton, Richmal (1951), *William Carries On*, London: George Newnes and Sydney: Dymock's Book Arcade, pp. 151–2. ·
16   Solow, Robert M. (1970), 'Science and Ideology in Economics', *The Public Interest*, Fall, reprinted in *Readings in Economics '73/'74* (1973), Guilford, CT.: Annual Editions, p. 11.
17   Smith, Adam (1982), *The Theory of Moral Sentiments*, Indianapolis: Liberty Classics.
18   Handy, C. (1994), *The Empty Raincoat*, London: Hutchinson, p. 15. Similar sentiments are expressed by Mark Garnett who argues that the liberal values of John Stuart Mill who prized altruism have been replaced in the post-Thatcher era with a 'hollowed out', Hobbesian philosophy which gives a central place to self-interest. See Gray, John (2004),

'Trouble at Mill', *Australian Financial Review*, 19 November, p. 10, reprinted from *The New Statesman.*

19 Marshall, Alfred (1920), *Principles of Economics*, 8th ed., London: Macmillan, p. 637. In a cautionary footnote to this paragraph, Marshall remarks that Mill made 'excessive claims for the deductive method in economics.' Nonetheless, his practice, says Marshall, 'was less extreme than his profession.'

20 See, for example, Hayden, Anders (1999), *Sharing the Work, Sparing the Planet*, London: Zed Books, pp. 80–5 and pp. 168–69. Although he recites this argument he appears to be aware that it is untenable.

21 An anonymous reviewer has prompted me to say that it should not be inferred from this statement that the author is unaware of, or unsympathetic to, the reservations held by many about the claims of economics to be value free.

22 Beckerman, Wilfred (1991), 'Global Warming: a Sceptical Economic Assessment', Chap. 3 in Helm, D. (ed.), *Economic policy towards the environment*, Oxford: Blackwell, pp. 52–85.

23 Even some of the economic literature contains the suggestion that this frailty – in the form of an addiction to consumption – is the root cause of the problem. See, for example, Booth, D. (2004), *Hooked on Growth: Economic Addictions and the Environment*, Lanham, MD: Rowman and Littlefield.

24 Kaufman, B.E. (1999), 'Expanding the Behavioural Foundations of Labor Economics', *Industrial and Labor Relations Review*, **52** (3), p. 386.

25 Baumol, W.J. and Quandt, R.E. (1964), 'Rules of Thumb and Optimally Imperfect Decisions', *American Economic Review*, **43**, pp. 23–4.

26 See, for example, Schor, Juliet (1992), *The Overworked American*, New York: Basic Books.

27 Mills, M. (2003), *The Scheme for Full Employment*, London: Flamingo, pp. 87–8.

28 Fukuyama, Francis (1992), *The End of History and the Last Man*, London: Penguin.

29 See, for example, Hayden (1999), pp. 31–41.

30 For some estimates of the enormous subjective costs of unemployment see Layard, Richard (2005), *Happinesss*, New York: Penguin.

31 The lack of hard evidence is discussed in Douthwaite (1999).

32 An interesting aspect of the relationship between congestion and travel time is the suggestion by labour economist Daniel Hamermesh that the growing concentration of work on the periphery of the 'normal' working day may result from commuters travelling to or from work at off-peak times in order to reduce the congestion costs they incur. See Hamermesh, Daniel (1998), 'When We Work', *American Economic Review*, **88** (2), p. 323.

33 From a letter; quoted in Noble, A. (ed.) (2000), *The Little Book of Sayings of Oscar Wilde*, Bath: Parragon, p. 94.

2. The Fundamental Flaw

*[I]ncreases in output undermine precisely those factors which **do** yield welfare. Here I have in mind the growing worktime requirements of the market economy, and the concomitant decline in family, leisure, and community time; the adverse impacts of growth on the natural environment; and the potential link between growth and social capital.*[1]

Juliet Schor

In this chapter we first examine the economics of the-trade off between work and leisure – how the appropriate work-life balance is determined. This analysis helps to explain the conundrum of recent increases in work time in many countries in the context of the enormous decrease in lifetime work hours that has occurred in these same countries over the past century. Having discussed some economic explanations for these trends, in the second part of the chapter we explain that, *no matter to what extent work hours may have decreased over the past century,* a fundamental flaw in the capitalist system causes the amount of work undertaken by citizens to be excessive. Furthermore, it will be shown later in Chapter 6 that this situation has prevailed in the West since the commencement of the industrial revolution.

THE DEMARCATION BETWEEN WORK AND LEISURE

Why do we go to work? Do we work to earn the income needed to feed, clothe, entertain and educate ourselves and our families; to give us the prestige that a good job confers; to give us a network of friends and colleagues; or is it to enable us to escape the drudgery of home-based productive activities?[2] For most of us the idea that we will work for much of our adult life is instilled in us from an early age. But we all know that all work and no play makes Jack a dull boy. Thus we choose to spend only some of any given time period engaged in work as opposed to rest or leisure. More than half a century ago, the labour movement's agitation for division of the day into 8 hours work, 8 hours play and 8 hours rest was successful. Today, for most workers in developed countries, the working week is limited to 5 days, and the working year consists of 48 to 50 weeks of work less public holidays. Not only has the total number of hours worked each year decreased significantly but with more time spent at school, with retirement occurring at an earlier age and with increased life expectancy, participation in the workforce is now restricted to little more than half a person's lifetime. By contrast, participation of women in the formalized work force has increased enormously over the past four decades.

So what determines the extent to which individuals spend time working as opposed to engaging in rest or leisure? If we assume that a certain amount of rest is biologically and psychologically necessary for a healthy human existence, and that humans choose to have this amount of rest – notwithstanding the assertions from some quarters that sleep deprivation is the bane of modern civilization – this question becomes one of determining how individuals decide to divide their available time between work and leisure.[3] At this stage we shall describe all time not spent on the job or asleep as leisure. Later in this chapter, we shall briefly discuss the allocation of this leisure time between activities that might be described as home-based work and those that come under the category of play. It is worth mentioning, in passing, that in their inimitable style economists have given consideration to the trade-off between sleep and other activities that might substitute for it; in the analysis presented here it is assumed that no loss of rigour results from ignoring any such trade-off.[4]

This distinct division of the day into work time given over to one's employer and leisure time of one's own is, as the historian E.P. Thompson has pointed out, a relatively recent phenomenon which first appeared when employers paid for their employee's time rather than for completion of a particular task. He explains the significance of the division of the day in the following way.

> This measurement [of time] embodies a simple relationship. Those who are employed experience a distinction between their employer's time and their "own" time. And the employer must *use* [original emphasis] the time of his labour, and see it is not wasted: not the task but the value of time when reduced to money is dominant.[5]

No one could have better explained the importance to the individual of this division than did Benjamin Franklin in his advice to a young tradesman:

> Remember that TIME is Money. He that can earn Ten Shillings a Day by his Labour, and goes abroad, or sits idle one half of that Day, tho' he spends but Sixpence during his Diversion or Idleness, ought not to reckon That the only Expence; he has really spent or rather thrown away Five Shillings besides.[6]

Given that, for most people, the day is clearly demarcated into work time and leisure time, what determines the ratio between them?

THE ALLOCATION OF TIME

From the perspective of the liberal economic tradition, the allocation of time between work and leisure is determined by the trade-off between work which involves the sacrifice of leisure and which is, on balance, seen as unpleasant, and the income we derive from work which enables us to engage in pleasurable consumption (or saving which allows for deferred consumption). Alfred Marshall explained the attainment of an equilibrium between work and pleasure in the following simple example.

> The simplest case of balance or equilibrium between desire and effort is found when a person satisfies one of his wants by his own direct work. When a boy picks blackberries for his own eating, the action of picking is probably itself pleasurable for a while; and for some time longer the pleasure of eating is more than enough to repay the trouble of picking. But after he has eaten a good deal, the desire for more diminishes; while the task of picking begins to cause weariness, which may indeed be a feeling of monotony rather than of fatigue. Equilibrium is reached when at last his eagerness to play and his disinclination for the work of picking counterbalance the desire for eating. The satisfaction which he can get from picking fruit has arrived at its maximum: for up to that time every fresh picking has added more to his pleasure than it has taken away; and after that time any further picking would take away from his pleasure more than it would add.[7]

From its utilitarian, individualistic perspective, economic theory sees the typical adult making a rational choice to forego pleasant leisure in order to engage in unpleasant work which brings with it the reward of consumption in all its manifold forms. As Scott Adams, the creator of Dilbert, has put it '[t]he only reason your company pays you is because you'd rather be doing something else.' He goes on: '[i]f you accept more unpleasantness, you can make more money. Likewise, you can often decrease the unpleasantness in your life by spending money to make it go away.'[8]

In case some fortunate readers with enjoyable jobs imagine that workers might typically find work pleasurable rather than unpleasurable, the evidence clearly shows that workers find work unpleasurable – and more so today than 50 years ago. In *Bowling Alone* Robert Putnam quotes Americans' responses to the Gallup poll question 'Which do you enjoy more, the hours when you are on your job, or the hours when you are not on your job?' Whereas, in 1955, some 44 per cent of workers said they enjoyed the hours on the job more, by 1999 only 16 per cent held this view.[9] The views of contemporary Americans echo those expressed by Mark Twain in *Tom Sawyer* more than a century ago: '[W]ork consists of whatever a body is obliged to do, and... Play consists of whatever a body is not obliged to do.'[10]

Putnam also provides evidence, consistent with the often espoused argument provided by women, that increased participation of women in the workforce is, to put it bluntly, a matter of necessity rather than choice. In the late 1990s, roughly three times as many women in full-time employment said they work for financial reasons as said they worked for personal satisfaction.[11] Nonetheless, it should be emphasized that the liberal economic position is that these women chose voluntarily to enter the workforce believing that the benefits of their participation would outweigh the costs, resulting in a net gain.

The non-economist may object that the motivation to endure displeasure by engaging in work in free societies is a far more complex matter than one of simply enabling consumption. Indeed, factors such as habit, the work ethic, and a desire to raise the welfare of fellow members of society are very important.[12] Nonetheless, it is clear that if these factors are taken as given and are acknowledged to be outside the purview of the economic analysis being undertaken here, the major motivating factor behind our work effort is the desire to consume. As pointed out in Chapter 1, changes in society's underlying values that might come about as a result of education, religion or propaganda are seen by some as providing a way of reducing our demands upon the environment. Yet, there is little evidence that this is possible. Consistent with the liberal economic tradition, and in order to concentrate on the work, leisure trade-off, it is assumed here that society's underlying value system is given. That is, factors such as habit, the work ethic or the desire to help others are assumed to have an influence that changes only slowly over time.

This is not to imply that different individuals do not have different attitudes to the relative benefits of consumption as opposed to the costs of engaging in work. It means only that the amount of work undertaken by a country's citizens will, all other factors remaining constant, be determined by the amount of income (consumption potential) that is received as compensation for this work. In arguing that consumption is the sole motivation for work we are in the good company of the two most important economists of the modern era – Adam Smith and John Maynard Keynes – both of whom argued that consumption is the sole purpose of economic activity. Renowned economist Meghnad Desai argues that all economists accept this proposition:

> Economists take it as a 'self evident truth' that consumption is the end of all economic activity. Accumulation of wealth, economic growth, and increasing productivity are all seen ultimately as justified if they promise a higher level of consumption per capita in the future than the 'society' enjoys in the present.[13]

Furthermore, he goes on to explain that '…it is always assumed that the individual will always want more goods – there is no satiety in the economist's world.'[14] Nonetheless, it should be emphasized at this stage that consumption by individuals can take many forms – including consumption of goods and services provided by the state and funded by taxes levied on income or expenditure. When it is said that the sole purpose of economic activity is consumption, this consumption is not confined to that of goods and services privately produced and traded in markets. The importance of consumption of goods and services provided by the state as a factor affecting individual work effort will become apparent as our explanation of the determinants of work effort unfolds.

Consumption may well be the sole purpose of economic activity in capitalist democracies but, as environmental researcher and campaigner Alan Thein Durning points out, this irresistible desire to consume more does not necessarily result in fulfilment:

> If human desires are in fact infinitely expandable, consumption is ultimately incapable of providing fulfilment – a logical consequence ignored by economic theory. Indeed social scientists have found striking evidence that high-consumption societies, just as high-living individuals, consume ever more without achieving satisfaction. The allure of the consumer society is powerful, even irresistible, but it is shallow nonetheless.[15]

Notwithstanding the central role in economic theory of consumption as the basis for work, we should be clear in our understanding that consumption is not the sole purpose of *life* which can be enhanced by more leisure and fewer material pursuits. In his 'Economic Possibilities for our Grandchildren' John Maynard Keynes foresaw an era in which the fruits of economic progress would shift the emphasis from consumption to that of living a life:

> The strenuous purposeful money-makers may carry all of us along with them into the lap of economic abundance. But it will be those peoples, who can keep alive, and cultivate into a fuller perfection, the art of life itself and do not sell themselves for the means of life, who will be able to enjoy the abundance when it comes.[16]

We now turn to a discussion of the ways in which changes in factors such as unpleasantness of work, quality of life and remuneration affect work effort.

CHOOSING THE RIGHT LEVEL OF WORK EFFORT

At any given point in time, a decrease in the unpleasantness of work (for the same pay) is likely to increase the amount of work undertaken, resulting in a concomitant decrease in leisure time. This is consistent with the idea that people who enjoy their work more (dislike it less) are likely to work longer hours. This is said to be the case in many professional occupations.[17] Following similar logic, an increase in remuneration for a job involving a given amount of unpleasantness will result in more work and less leisure. The tendency for individuals to substitute work for leisure as income increases is described by economists as the *substitution effect*.

To see why there is a tendency to substitute work for leisure when income increases, consider the rate of pay per hour that would entice you to take on an extra job for, say, four hours per week. Would you do it for $15 per hour, $20 per hour, $40 per hour, $100 per hour, $200 per hour or would you need to be paid even more? The likelihood that you would take up the job rises as the prospective rate of pay increases. As the rate of remuneration rises you will increase your work effort.[18] It is this idea that is behind the widely accepted argument that income taxes should be reduced because they discourage work effort. As we shall see later in Chapter 7, although this is a widely accepted argument, when consideration is given to the way in which government spends these taxes, it may be found to be incorrect.

But substitution of work for leisure as the unpleasantness of work decreases and as the monetary reward for working increases tells only part of the story. In spite of recent trends to more annual work hours and less leisure in some countries, it remains that over the course of the past century there has been a marked reduction in hours worked per day, per year, and throughout a lifetime. The best way to understand this phenomenon is to think of leisure as a luxury. Economists have studied extensively the effect of changes in our income on our consumption of different goods and services. As our incomes rise we tend to consume more goods and services that we class as luxuries and fewer goods and services that we consider to be inferior. Thus as our incomes rise we consume more designer label clothes and fewer generic clothes. Leisure is like designer label clothes – as our income goes up over time we desire to 'consume' more leisure. The tendency for individuals to desire more leisure as income increases is described by economists as the *income effect*.

So with rising rates of pay over time we see two opposing forces – on the one hand the substitution effect tilts the trade-off between work and leisure in favour of work because it can now buy us more consumption goods, but on the other hand the income effect sees the rise in income causing us to demand more of the luxury of leisure time. Because the tendency over the long haul has been for leisure to increase as incomes have increased, economists tend to argue that the income effect is stronger than the substitution effect. A study by Ausubel and Gruebler into allocation of lifetime hours in the UK shows that over the past 150 years the percentage of disposable time allocated to work by the population has fallen from approximately 50 per cent to just 20 per cent.[19] In a similar vein, a US study has estimated that in the 120 years from 1870 to 1990, American's 'waking leisure' has increased threefold.[20] Given this long-run experience, why then has there been a recent, and much lamented, tendency for annual work hours to increase and leisure to decrease in some countries, particularly, as Juliet Schor has shown, in the US?[21] Four possible explanations based on an economic understanding of the motivation to work come to mind:

1. Work has become less unpleasant. The decrease in unpleasantness of work and working conditions that has occurred over the past quarter of a

century would, all other factors remaining constant, tilt the trade-off between work and leisure towards more work.[22]

2. Incomes have increased. Through the substitution effect, the modest rise in work-related incomes in the past quarter of a century would also encourage substitution of work for leisure.

3. Quality of life has fallen. If the income effect that would normally be expected to result in a reduction in work hours as incomes have increased is negated by declining quality of life (QOL), workers may choose to work longer hours to compensate for such a decline.

4. Workers have reallocated their work time. Workers may be choosing to work longer hours when they are in their prime but, given that they are entering the workforce later and retiring earlier they may, nonetheless, work fewer hours in a lifetime.

As to the third explanation, it has been shown that rising incomes could be expected to encourage workers to work less because they treat leisure as a luxury they can now more easily afford. So, in recent times, why hasn't this income effect outweighed the tendency for individuals to substitute work for leisure as a result of increased incomes and decreased unpleasantness of work? After all, this is what seems to have happened over the long haul. As will be argued at greater length in Chapter 5, the answer may be that recent rises in income have masked a significant decrease in QOL which has *encouraged* increased work effort. If the effect of this decrease in QOL is to make individuals feel poorer – in spite of increases in their incomes – then they would work longer hours because they feel that they are less able to afford the luxury of leisure. The question of the extent to which our incomes and our QOL have diverged over recent decades is taken up later in Chapter 5. In Chapter 7 it is conjectured that differences in the extent of this divergence on different sides of the Atlantic may help explain the longer working hours in the US as compared to Europe.

The fourth explanation given above involves what economists describe as intertemporal labor substitution. It relies on the idea that when workers are in their prime and their productivity and remuneration per hour are highest they will increase their work hours.[23] To compensate for this increased work effort in their prime they would reduce work hours when their productivity and resulting remuneration are low. Of course, worker productivity and earnings tend to decrease with age beyond the mid-life prime years. Thus we may be observing a tendency for workers to work long hours while they are employed but choosing to limit the duration of their working life by retiring early, leaving decades of leisure time to be enjoyed before departing this world. Taken with increased life expectancy and the tendency for individuals to increasingly postpone entry into the workforce until income-enhancing education has been undertaken, this tendency for individuals to retire early means that individuals are in the workforce for an increasingly declining

proportion of their life span.[24] Recent studies which reveal that workers are
working longer annual hours than previously would thus only indicate an
increased preference for work over leisure if it could be established that the
workers who are observed to be working longer hours today are not
compensating for this increased work effort by reducing the proportion of
their lifetime in the workforce.

In summary, from an economic perspective, the factors that might have
encouraged increased work effort over the past quarter of a century are:
decreased unpleasantness of work; increased incomes; declining QOL; and
intertemporal labour substitution.[25]

Another more complex factor that might lead to a choice of increased work
in the face of increased incomes would be a tendency for workers to
endeavour to increase the pleasure derived from leisure time by increasing
the consumption goods and services that are complementary to it. All other
factors remaining constant, this increased consumption of complementary
goods and services can only be achieved by an increase in the ratio of work
time to leisure time. Jonathan Gershuny explains this possibility in the
following way:

> [B]y working longer hours, we can earn more money, which we can spend to make
> our leisure time more intensely enjoyable. We work more and have less leisure. But
> the shorter leisure time, when combined with the extra money we can spend on it,
> provides us with more satisfaction in total than we might alternatively have gained
> by taking more leisure combined with less money.[26]

For example, it might be rational for an individual to work longer hours so as
to afford a short, expensive vacation spent overseas rather than work fewer
hours but have a longer, cheaper vacation spent at home. This approach
might be dubbed the 'work hard, play hard model'. Commenting on the
demise of the short-hour movements between the wars, historian Gary Cross
argues that the desire to substitute income generating work for leisure was an
important contributing factor:

> This did not end the dream of weekend leisure or the holiday with pay. But these
> periods of time free from work were increasingly devoted to consumption and thus
> were constrained by demands for income-producing work.[27]

This possible explanation for increases in work hours, such as have occurred
in recent decades in countries like the US, indicates the complexity involved
in making the appropriate choice between paid work and leisure. However, it
in no way alters the fundamental proposition that the level of work effort is
determined by the trade-off between unpleasant work and the income it
provides. Furthermore, there is no evidence that this 'work hard, play hard'
explanation is more relevant today than it might have been half a century or a
century ago. The advent of train travel, the motor vehicle, air travel, holiday

resorts and a host of other complements for leisure time have provided a continuous stimulus to leisure-based consumption over the past century or more; at the same time, there has been an enormous decrease in the proportion of our lifetime waking hours devoted to work.

The basic economic approach to the determination of the work, leisure trade-off is straightforward. At any time, the amount of work – and thus leisure – that we engage in is determined by a decision to weigh the benefits of work in the form of income against its costs in the form of unpleasantness. The liberal economic position is that the amount of work each of us undertakes is not a matter of serendipity or administrative fiat or necessity; it is a matter of free choice.

In taking this position, it is acknowledged that this analysis stands in stark contrast to the work of many authors who have written about the work, leisure trade-off. In particular, it is very different from the position taken by Juliet Schor in her book *The Overworked American*.[28] Schor, a former Harvard economist whose work in this area belongs to the institutional school of economics rather than the mainstream, asserts that we have little choice with respect to work hours.[29] Rather than taking the mainstream position that, in respect of work hours, workers 'get what they want', she argues that, in fact, because employers have the whip hand, workers 'want what they get'.[30] Elsewhere in the book, Schor unintentionally counters this argument by pointing out that some workers choose to work at a number of jobs to make ends meet; she also catalogues the enormous (threefold) increase in participation of married women in the workforce in the US over the past half of a century. Each of these phenomena is hardly a case of workers 'wanting what they get'. In Europe, as we shall see in Chapter 7, both hours of work and participation rates, especially those of married women, are much lower than in the US. Is this what European employers are serving up to their employees and potential employees who 'want what they get'?

Economists are aware that in the short term, the degree of individual choice regarding working hours is constrained by labour laws and bargaining between employers and groups of employees. Labour economist Lonnie Golden quotes survey evidence which shows that 'preferences concerning weekly hours vary considerably among individuals, but few jobs permit marginal adjustment of weekly hours along a continuous labor supply function.'[31] Although this constraint may be limited in the case of casual workers who can vary hours and number of jobs, it is often binding for salaried employees who find that they may have no choice but to work each week for no less than the number of hours determined by these arrangements. This constraint notwithstanding, it is clear that over the long term, the number of hours worked per week, per year, and per lifetime has fallen dramatically. In the period from 1870 to 1992 the number of hours worked per person employed in the US fell by a staggering 46 per cent.[32] Thus, although the individual salaried employee may not be in a position to choose shorter working hours today, over the long haul we have seen a significant substitution of leisure for work as incomes have risen and collective demands for shorter working hours have been met.[33] But has the reduction in working hours gone far enough or does the fundamental flaw in the system which was introduced in Chapter 1 cause us to work longer hours than we should, and consume more than we should?

In the opening paragraph of this chapter it was explained that although it would be argued in the first part of the chapter that the *increase* in annual work hours observed in recent times may be explained as having a sound economic basis, this does not preclude the possibility that the *level* of work hours undertaken by workers at any given time is, nonetheless, excessive. In the next section, the fundamental flaw in the system that does, indeed, cause excess work hours is explained.

THE FUNDAMENTAL FLAW IN THE SYSTEM

Notwithstanding the long-run tendency for life time work hours to fall, if the current choice of the amount of time devoted to leisure − as opposed to work − is biased towards work because there is some fundamental flaw in the economic system, this means that individuals are destroying work-life balance by voluntarily engaging in longer hours of work than would maximize their well-being. It is a central argument in this book that there is such a fundamental flaw, and that this flaw both results from, and leads to, excessive demands on the environment. The term 'excessive' in this context implies that the calls that we make upon the environment are such that they lead to a lower level of well-being than could otherwise be achieved. In other words, if our decision-making was not flawed, we would choose to work fewer hours, enjoy more leisure and experience far greater environmental amenity. For simple-minded protagonists of free market capitalism, the laissez-faire economy cannot be characterized by such a fundamental flaw. These simple-minded theorists ignore the economist's concept of market failure which describes real world situations where nonconformity to the simple model of laissez-faire results in free markets giving less than optimal outcomes.

These market failures are many and varied. They include:

- *information limitations* which, for example, may cause one party in a trade to be advantaged by having access to more, or better, information than the other;
- *public goods* which are not produced by the private sector because, in spite of their benefit to the community, it is not profitable to produce them;

- *natural monopoly* that results in firms being freed from the constraints of competition; and
- *externalities* that cause benefit or harm to third parties when two parties freely engage in market transactions.

Of these market failures, it is externalities (sometimes euphemistically described as spillovers) that are central to our argument that a flawed system causes us to choose an excess of work over leisure with devastating effects on the environment. In particular, we concentrate on *negative externalities* that cause harm to third parties when two parties engage in market transactions.

NEGATIVE EXTERNALITIES

Some typical examples of negative externalities that impact on environmental amenity include: the pollution from factories that occurs when they produce products for consumers or other producers; loss of biodiversity that occurs when agricultural activities designed to ultimately satisfy consumer demand degrade natural assets; and the vast range of productive activities that contribute to global warming. These are all examples of *production externalities* – they occur when the production of goods confers a cost upon parties other than those that produce or consume these goods.

In addition to these production externalities, there are also environmentally damaging *consumption externalities*. These occur when consumption of a good has an adverse effect on a party who was not a participant in the market transaction that lead to the purchase of the good by the consumer from a producer. Examples include air pollution caused by the use of petrol in motor cars, noise pollution emanating from homes or live music venues, and the environmental costs of urban sprawl resulting from consumption of housing. As we shall explain further in the next chapter, the costs that these negative externalities (of both types) impose on individuals do not normally enter the calculus of the work, leisure trade-off. The result is that contemporary liberal democracies are characterized by too much work and too little leisure. Too much work and too little leisure means, of course, too much production, too much consumption and too much environmental disamenity.

Lest it be thought that the concept of externalities is a recent one it should be pointed out that they have been recognized – if not characterized as externalities – since the beginnings of human interaction. They have also been recognized by economists as having importance as impediments to the efficient working of market economies since the birth of modern economics in the 18th century. As early as the 1920s, the English economist Arthur Pigou recommended taxes on activities that result in significant negative externalities as a way of reducing their incidence by imposing the cost of the externality on the responsible party. It is, however, only in the past 30 years or so that economists have widely acknowledged the significance of externalities, and developed a wide range of economic policies designed to reduce or eliminate them. As John Kenneth Galbraith has noted, up until that time, '[t]he noninclusion of external diseconomies was long viewed as a minor defect of the price system – an afterthought for an hour's classroom discussion.'[34] When one considers that the earth's finite resources are set against exponential growth in population and output, it is no wonder that these externalities loom larger today than ever before. Some 30 years ago one of the giants of the economics discipline, Robert Solow, warned that when externalities are important, the market might not work so well '…and other, more directly political, decision methods may take its place.'[35] He went on:

> The trouble is that each producer and consumer compares the market price with benefits to himself; other benefits and costs are not taken into anyone's account…. As standards of living rise, population density increases, and technological interactions grow more pervasive, it may be that a greater and greater part of economic life will have to come under these rules of the game, which may turn out to be quite different from the rules of the private-property game. [36]

Consistent with Solow's predictions, the capacity of the atmosphere to assimilate further pollution, the capacity of forests and fisheries to cope with increased rates of harvesting, and the capacity of cities to accommodate increased population are all now pressing against previously unforseen limits. In other words, these negative externalities – these unintended adverse effects on third parties – are now more important than ever before. What is more, as was pointed out in the previous chapter, it is the rich countries of the world that make the greatest per capita contribution to these negative externalities. This is borne out by the research undertaken by researchers at Redefining Progress. This organization estimates the call that different nations make on the world environment by looking at the amount of the world's biological productivity the average person uses in each country. They describe this call on the environment the 'ecological footprint'.

ECOLOGICAL FOOTPRINTS

In 2000 Redefining Progress estimated that across all countries, the ecological footprint was 20 per cent in excess of the earth's biological capacity – the capacity that sets the upper bound to sustainability. While some poor countries such as Pakistan, Ethiopia, Tajikistan, Mozambique and Bangladesh have per capita footprints that are less than a third of the world average, the per capita footprint for the US is over four times the average. European countries typically have per capita footprints that are about double the average, as does Japan. The per capita footprint for Australasia is over three times the world average while those of the world's most populous nations – India and China – are one-third and two-thirds of the world average respectively.[37] In measuring the call per capita that each nation makes on the environment, Redefining Progress looks at the use of environmental resources attributable to that country no matter whether or not the resources used are located in the country itself. Thus a country like the UK which has a small endowment of natural resources per capita, has a per capita footprint that is more than twice the global average. More than half its per capita call on the environment is enabled by external environmental resources comprising common global resources or resources in other countries from which it imports goods and services. Even the US with its large endowment of natural resources makes a per capita call on external resources that constitutes almost half of its total per capita footprint.

As we shall see in the next chapter, these ecological footprints can be used to show that it is possible for a reduction in work hours to be accompanied by a very significant reduction in environmental degradation.

APPROACHING THE PROBLEM FROM THE RIGHT STANDPOINT

Over a century ago, Thorstein Veblen railed against the evils of conspicuous consumption; nearly half a century ago following the intercession of two world wars and the Great Depression, John Kenneth Galbraith attacked the consumerism of the affluent society. Today the genre is perpetuated in books and television programmes, the best known example of which may be the KCTS/Seattle and Oregon Public Broadcasting *Affluenza* documentaries. But why, after more than a century of persuasive argument against the consumer society, are we still facing the same problem of over consumption? The answer is that we have been attacking the problem from the wrong standpoint. So long as we continue to promote individual liberty in democratic capitalist societies, human beings acting of their own free-will are going to consume – either now or later – all of the output the economy produces. Calls to lower our levels of consumption will not be heeded – as 100 years of evidence attests. The correct standpoint from which to attack the problem involves looking at the *source* of the capacity for consumption by individuals. This source is the work effort put in by those individuals. Although the 20th century was characterized by significant declines in the number of lifetime hours worked by individuals, it remains that at any given time during that century – Great Depression and World War years excepted – the fundamental flaw resulted in work hours being excessive.

The basic argument put forward here is that individuals are, of their own free-will, working longer hours than would maximize their happiness. They do this because the fundamental flaw in the economy prevents them from correctly assessing the benefits they derive from their work effort. Because they overestimate the benefits of their work effort by looking at the consumption goods it buys rather than the combination of consumption goods it buys and the negative externalities that are produced, they work longer hours than they should.

Early on in this chapter it was explained that although all time not spent on the job or asleep would be described as leisure, there would be a later discussion of the allocation of this leisure time between activities that might be described as home-based work and those that come under the category of play. We look at this allocation in the next section.

THE ALLOCATION OF LEISURE TIME

The analysis being undertaken in this book looks exclusively at the trade-off between paid work and leisure. A richer treatment of the relationship between work and leisure has been developed by Mario Cogoy.[38] Although this treatment is not used here, it does clarify the choices made by individuals, and it does enable us to see that the simpler approach taken here is adequate to our task. Cogoy makes a tripartite division of waking time which can be spent as:

1.   production time (paid work);
2.   consumption time (unpaid work);
3.   enjoyment time.

This simple model sees individuals as working in the work place to earn income that buys consumption goods and services that can be used for their own sake in enjoyment time, or which can be an input into a home-based work activity that produces output that can ultimately be used in enjoyment time. As an example of the use of consumption goods for their own sake, consider the individual who engages in paid work to enable the purchase of a tennis racquet that is used directly in enjoyment time. An example using consumption goods in conjunction with unpaid work would be the use of the proceeds of paid work to purchase cleaning agents so that they can be transformed as a result of unpaid work into a clean home that is consumed in enjoyment time. In this model, the trade-off is between the displeasure of paid and unpaid work on the one hand and the pleasure of enjoyment time on the other. Despite its richness, this model uses a degree of complexity that is not required here. For our purposes, a simple division of waking time into paid work and leisure (which includes both unpaid work and enjoyment time) is sufficient.

The reason that little emphasis is given to the question of how leisure time is divided between home-based work activities and enjoyment time is that home-based work activities are generally far more environmentally benign than work-based activities. That is, they provide far fewer, and less costly, negative externalities. The major reason for this is that many ill-effects of home-based work activities are likely to be felt by householders themselves and traced to the offending home-based activity. Remedial action is then likely to be taken. With few home-based negative externalities to consider, the way in which people divide their leisure time between home-based work and play is not subject to the fundamental flaw – what people do in their leisure time is their business.[39] By contrast, in deciding between environmentally malignant paid work and the alternative of relatively benign leisure, our decision is severely distorted by the fundamental flaw – the way in which people divide their time between paid work and leisure is everybody's business. As a corollary to this conclusion, it is likely that individuals have a bias towards work in the work place as opposed to home-based work because the transference of work from home to the work place removes the ill-effects of this work from the home. This bias is reinforced by legislation which prohibits noisy or polluting activities in residential areas. Insofar as the ill-effects are corralled in locations zoned for business activity, this transference is a good thing. However, to the extent that this transference severs the link between an individual's work activities and the negative externalities they cause it is a bad thing; for it is this severance of the link between work and the negative externalities it creates that is the root cause of the fundamental flaw.

In the next chapter we take a closer look at the effects of these environmentally damaging negative externalities on the work, leisure trade-off in contemporary society. The last word has been variously attributed to Charlie McCarthy, Edgar Bergen and Ronald Reagan:

They say hard work never hurt anybody, but I figure why take the chance.

NOTES

1   Schor, J., 'The New Politics of Consumption', at http://www-polisci.mit.edu /BR24.3 /schor/html, p. 10 accessed 13 July 2004.
2   I am indebted to an anonymous reviewer who has pointed me in the direction of Nobel Prize-winning economist Amartya Sen's distinction between three different aspects of employment: its income earning aspect, its production aspect, and the aspect involving its capacity to give persons recognition as being involved in something worth while. See Sen, Amartya, (1999), *Employment, Technology and Development*, Oxford University Press, New Delhi, Chap. 1. As is made clear below, without wanting to diminish the importance of the third aspect, this work is concerned only with variations in the first two.
3   A measure of the extent to which there is concern that sleep deprivation is a serious problem is found in the 5 500 000 hits made when the term 'sleep deprivation' was entered into a popular search engine in late 2005.
4   An economic approach to sleep deprivation would explore the extent to which incentives can encourage the substitution of waking time for time asleep. See Biddle, J.E. and

Hamermesh, D.S. (1990), 'Sleep and the Allocation of Time', *Journal of Political Economy*, **98** (5), pp. 922–43.

5   Thompson, E.P. (1967), 'Time, Work-discipline, and Industrial Capitalism', *Past and Present,* **38**, p. 60.

6   Franklin, Benjamin (1748), 'Advice to a Young Tradesman, Written by an Old One', at http://www.historycarper.com/resources/twobf2/advice.htm, accessed 14 June 2006.

7   Marshall, Alfred (1920), *Principles of Economics*, 8th ed., London: Macmillan, p. 276.

8   Adams, S. (1998), *The joy of work: Dilbert's guide to finding happiness at the expense of your co-workers*, New York: HarperCollins, p. 12.

9   Putnam, R.D. (2000), *Bowling Alone*, New York: Simon & Schuster, p. 91.

10   Twain, Mark (1950), *Tom Sawyer*, Puffin Books, pp. 19–20.

11   Putnam, (2000), p. 198, Fig. 48.

12   Discussion of the broader motivation to work can be found in Fukuyama, Francis (1992), *The End of History and the Last Man*, London: Penguin, Chap. 21 and Smith, Tom W. (2000), 'A Cross-national Comparison on Attitudes towards Work by Age and Labor Force Status', OECD report at http://www.oecd.org/LongAbstract/0,2546,en_2649_33729_2535795_119666_1_1_37457,00.html, accessed 27 January 2006.

13   Desai, M. (1977), 'Consumption and pollution', in Hirst, I.R.C. and Duncan Reekie (eds) (1977), *The Consumer Society*, London: Tavistock Publications, pp. 22–36.

14   Ibid.

15   Durning, A.T. (1992), 'The Dubious Rewards of Consumption', *New Renaissance Magazine*, **3** (2), p. 2.

16   Keynes, J.M. (1972), 'Economic Possibilities for Our Grandchildren', from *Essays in Persuasion*, being Volume XI of *The Collected Works of John Maynard Keynes*, London: Macmillan, p. 328.

17   Scitovsky, Tibor (1976), *The Joyless Economy*, Oxford: Oxford University Press, pp. 93–96. For a contemporary sociological take on this see Bunting, Madeleine (2004), *Willing Slaves*, London: HarperCollins, pp. 164–73.

18   I am indebted to Ted Kolsen who has reminded me that this tendency is manifested in the need for employers to pay workers at a higher rate in order to have them work overtime.

19   Quoted in Nordhaus, W.D. (2000), 'New Directions in National Economic Accounting', *American Economic Review*, **90** (2), p. 261, Fig. 1.

20   Cox and Alm quoted in McKenzie, R.B. (1997), *The Paradox of Progress*, New York: Oxford University Press, p. 70.

21   Schor, Juliet (1992), *The Overworked American*, New York: Basic Books. It appears that this problem can be associated particularly with English-speaking countries. The most prominent recent addition to the literature dealing with overwork comes from British journalist Madeleine Bunting who notes that overwork is also a characteristic of Australia and New Zealand. See Bunting, *Willing Slaves*, p. 302.

22   Scitovsky cites historical evidence showing that, over time, professionals who have control over the hours that they work tended to increase their work hours. See Scitovsky (1976), pp. 99–100.

23   Perhaps the best-known application of intertemporal labour substitution is the one found in real business cycle theory where it is used to explain why employment rises at times when wages are temporarily high. See Snowdon, B., Vane, H. and Wynarczyk, P. (1994), *A Modern Guide to Macroeconomics*, Aldershot, UK and Brookfield, US: Edward Elgar, pp. 247–8.

24   I have to thank Father John Barry for the following: 'The good news is that life expectancy has increased; the bad news is it's tacked on the end.'

25   Economist Lester Thurow in his *Zero-Sum Solution* attributes increased work hours primarily to an increase in the work ethic of Americans – their preferences have changed towards more work and less leisure. Such an attribution assumes away the question for which we are seeking an answer; namely, what has caused this change in preferences? See Thurow, Lester (1985), *The Zero-Sum Solution*, New York: Simon & Schuster, pp. 140–141. Former US labor secretary Robert Reich blames a range of factors, including

increased market competition between suppliers (including workers), for recent increases in work effort in the US. He paints a picture of work as a harried activity that is far less pleasant today than previously. However, as we have seen, economic theory suggests that if work becomes less pleasant (more unpleasant) we would be more likely to reduce our work effort than increase it. See Reich, Robert B. (2002), *The Future of Success*, USA: Vintage, Chap. 6.

26   Gershuny, J. (1992), 'Are We Running Out of Time?', *Futures*, January/February, p. 5.

27   Cross, G. (1993), *Time and Money*, London: Routledge, p. 11.

28   Schor (1992).

29   More recently Schor has become Professor of Sociology at Boston College.

30   Ibid, p. 127. It could be argued that Schor's position is supported by some contributions to behavioural economics that emphasize the importance for decision-making of the status quo (reference levels, endowment effects). Although some credence might be given to this argument in the short term, in the longer term dynamic economies are characterized by continual movement away from the status quo. Nowhere is this more apparent than in the massive reduction, over the past century or more, in the proportion of our lifetime waking hours that we spend at work.

31   Golden, L. (1990), 'The insensitive workweek: trends and determinants of adjustment in average hours', *Journal of Post Keynesian Economics*, **13** (1), p. 105.

32   Goklany, I.M. (2002), 'Economic growth and human well-being', Chap. 2 in Morris, J. (ed.), *Sustainable Development*, London: Profile Books, p. 31.

33   Consistent with her title, Madeleine Bunting, author of *Willing Slaves*, asserts that the British middle classes do have 'a degree of choice in how hard they work.' See Bunting, *Willing Slaves*, p.xxiii.

34   Galbraith, J.K. (1973) 'Power and the Useful Economist', *The American Economic Review*, March, reprinted in *Readings in Economics '73/'74* (1973), Guilford CT: Annual Editions, p. 19.

35   Solow, Robert M. (1970), 'Science and Ideology in Economics', *The Public Interest*, Fall, reprinted in *Readings in Economics '73/'74* (1973), Guilford, CT: Annual Editions, p. 11.

36   Ibid.

37   Venetoulis, J., Chazan, D. and Gaudet, C (2004), 'Ecological Footprint of Nations', Oakland, California: Redefining Progress.

38   Cogoy, M. (1999), 'The consumer as a social and environmental actor', *Ecological Economics*, **28**, pp. 385–98.

39   But, you might ask, don't activities undertaken in enjoyment time create negative externalities and won't these negative externalities grow if leisure is increased? The answer is that this will depend on the nature of the enjoyment time activities, and the extent to which an increase in their duration is countered by a reduction in their consumption intensity. That a leisure-seeking society will have more adverse effects on the environment than one that is hard working seems unlikely. Do the lifestyles of lazy individuals appear to generate more calls on the environment than those of hard workers? As Ng and Ng have put it: 'Income-earning work is related to production and consumption and leisure as such is less environmentally disruptive.' Ng, Y-K. and Ng, S. (2003), 'Do the economies of specialisation justify the work ethic?', *Journal of Economic Behaviour and Organization*, **50** (3), p. 350.

3. How Workers are Short-changed by Externalities

[I]f the economist is interested in social welfare rather than in physical output he must concern himself with the burden of this constraint on the worker's choice [of work hours] in a modern economy that is almost wholly consumer oriented – and, indeed, the private enterprise system is generally vindicated by reference to the individual's satisfaction qua *consumer while neglecting his satisfaction* qua *worker.*[1]

E.J. Mishan

Over the past half a century, the role that negative externalities play in the economy has come to be understood to a much greater extent than previously. In 1989, the OECD was able to say they were a former curiosum that was now recognized to be of great importance.[2] Externalities are a phenomenon that we all experience in our everyday lives although they may be more typically described as side-effects or unintentional side-effects. The reason that these side-effects or externalities have become better understood in recent years is the result of two factors. First, as we saw in the last chapter, the extent and magnitude of negative externalities has increased as population and economic activity have increased, while, at the same time, the capacity of the environment to accommodate them has decreased. Second, recognizing the increased importance of negative externalities, economists have developed an enormous number of theoretical approaches to deal with them and to underpin policies that might ameliorate their effects. Whether it be taxes on pollutants, tradeable permits for fishing rights or CO_2 emissions, charges for previously unpriced water, or incentives for the recycling of beverage containers, the influence of economists in endeavouring to control externalities are seen all around us.

In spite of the good intentions of environmentalists, economists and governments, these policies have only scratched the surface of the problem in developed countries; and they have been of even less relevance in developing countries. Negative externalities that degrade the environment are a bigger problem today than they have ever been. To be sure, some progress has been made – especially in rich countries. Lead has been removed from gasoline; logging of old growth forests has been curtailed; SO_2 emissions have been reduced; and so on. But catastrophes on the scale of Exxon Valdiz threaten, global warming continues, species depletion gathers pace, and urbanization and congestion grow. As developing countries become richer, their demands on the environment grow exponentially. More than a decade ago Alan Thein Durning explained how the 8 per cent of the world's population that then owned cars wrought havoc on their own communities and adversely affected the world environment:

> The auto class's fleet of four-wheelers is directly responsible for an estimated 13 percent of carbon dioxide emissions from fossil fuels worldwide, along with air pollution and acid rain, traffic fatalities numbering a quarter of a million annually, and the sprawl of urban areas into endless tract developments lacking community cohesion.

> The auto class bears indirect responsibility for the far-reaching impacts of their chosen vehicle. The automobile makes itself indispensable: cities sprawl, public transit atrophies, shopping centers multiply, employers scatter. Today, working Americans spend nine hours a week behind the wheel. To make these homes-away-from-home more comfortable, 90 percent of new American cars are air-conditioned, which adds emissions of gases that aggravate the greenhouse effect and deplete the ozone layer.[3]

We saw in the previous chapter that these negative externalities mean that when we work in order to earn income that enables us to consume, it is not just money income that we receive in return for our work effort. We also get pollution, congestion, loss of biodiversity and depletion of renewable and non-renewable resources that are the externalities from production and consumption of goods and services. Not only do these externalities affect us today but they also affect our children and our children's children. If we were to put a money value on these external costs and deduct them from money wages earned, we would find, as Chapter 5 will show, that workers are severely short-changed – the actual reward they receive for their work effort is significantly lower than the money wage they receive. Unfortunately, however, because of the fundamental flaw in the system, labour considers only the money wage it receives when deciding how much work effort to engage in.

Many negative externalities, like global warming, loss of biodiversity and depletion of forests, are not immediately apparent to workers in developed nations. However, anyone who has travelled in highly populated developing countries, where the extent of urban pollution is an affront to the senses, will have witnessed irrefutable evidence that there are very large external costs of production and consumption that should be set off against money income to determine the actual compensation workers receive for their work effort. When you hear friends or colleagues say that they wouldn't take up well-paid jobs in cities in these countries because of the ill-effects of urban pollution, you are witnessing an accounting for external costs that is seldom heard at home. Furthermore, the point needs to be made that much of the pollution caused by manufacturing production undertaken in developing countries adds to the ecological footprints of the developed countries to which a large part of this production is exported. We might not be willing to live in polluted cities in these countries but we happily engage in consumption of their goods, the production of which causes this pollution.

This separation of consumption decisions and the adverse effects they have on third parties in the linked commodity chain of resource-use decisions has been aptly described by environmental policy analyst Thomas Princen as *distancing*. Distancing is explained as:

> [T]he severing of ecological and social feedback as decision points along the chain are increasingly separated along the dimensions of geography, culture, agency, and power. Rather than viewing consumption as the exercise of consumer sovereignty in the context of perfect (or near-perfect) information, the concept of distancing highlights the increasingly isolated character of consumption choices as decision makers at individual nodes are cut off from a contextualized understanding of the ramifications of their choices, both upstream and downstream.[4]

In Chapter 2, it was pointed out that the potential for unpaid work hours in the home to be excessive is far less than in the case of paid work. This is because there is little potential for negative externalities to cause the fundamental flaw to operate in this context. Using his concept of distancing, Princen compares production and consumption by the individual or household with its market-based counterpart:

> At one extreme, zero-distance is production and consumption by one household or individual; at the other extreme, it is global, cross-cultural, and among agents of disparate abilities and alternatives.... [T]he environmental impacts of these consumption and production decisions are not always obvious, intended, or even known to decision makers.[5]

Up to this point, it has been negative externalities that have been emphasized as being at the heart of the fundamental flaw; but what about their counterpart – the positive externalities of production and consumption that confer unintended *benefits* upon third parties?

WHAT ABOUT POSITIVE EXTERNALITIES?

It is important to emphasize that there are positive externalities as well as negative externalities. Examples of positive externalities include the benefits to the community of decisions by individuals to immunize their children, the benefits of beautiful gardens to passers-by, and the benefits to existing users of networks, such as the Internet, that accompany decisions by other individuals to hook up – the so-called network externalities. As economists have pointed out, these positive externalities are likely to pale into insignificance as compared to negative externalities.[6] There are a number of reasons for this. First, profit-seeking entities have powerful incentives to try to capture the benefits of positive externalities (internalize them) so that they can be sold. Why let the fans watch the game for free when the field can be enclosed and an entrance fee charged? Second, if positive externalities of a firm's activities were large, but these firms were unable to charge for (capture) the benefits they confer on third parties, the sales revenues of these firms would be low in relation to their costs and it is likely that production of the output in question would not occur at all. This is the case of what economists call public goods which were mentioned in the previous chapter as an important case of market failure. Third, firms have an incentive to substitute negative externalities for internal costs because, by externalizing costs to third parties, they increase their profits. Why pay the costs of cleaning up pollution when it can be dumped on your neighbours?

Robert Putnam has put these ideas to good use in discussing work place practices that might help or hinder social capital formation. Putman contrasted the behaviour of firms when it comes to dealing with policies that increase positive externalities as compared to those that increase negative externalities.

> [M]any of the benefits of employment practices that encourage social capital formation − stronger families, more effective schools, safer neighbourhoods, more vibrant public life − 'leak' outside the firm itself, whereas all the costs stay put. This fact gives firms an incentive to underinvest in civic engagement by their employees. Conversely, workplace practices that inhibit community involvement and family connectedness produce a classic case of what economists term 'negative externalities', imposing an unrequited cost on society.[7]

In any event, to the extent that there *are* positive externalities from production or consumption, our money income will understate the benefits of our work effort. In an imaginary world in which there are positive externalities only, we would work too little because we would underestimate the benefits that accrue to our work effort.

When individuals gain benefits from positive externalities, they are described in the economics literature as taking a 'free ride'. This is a free ride to a desirable destination because the benefits they receive there are produced at no cost to themselves. On the other hand, when individuals suffer the costs of negative externalities we could say that they are on a 'forced ride'. This is a forced ride to somewhere they do not want to go − a place where they suffer costs with no compensating benefits. All of us are currently taking that forced ride; and, as we shall see shortly, there is no incentive for any of us to dismount.

MAXIMIZING HAPPINESS FROM WORK

The idea that because of the fundamental flaw we work longer hours than would maximize our well-being can be described using some simple graphs. The graphs that are described below look at the situation for the typical, or representative, person who is assumed to have the typical or representative level of income derived from work and to experience the typical or representative level of negative externalities in their everyday lives. Later in this chapter, some qualifications to this simple assumption will be discussed.

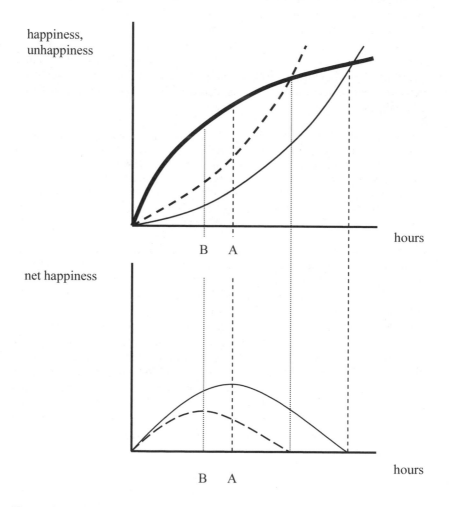

Figure 3.1   Maximizing happiness from work

In the upper graph of Figure 3.1 hours of work per week are shown on the horizontal axis. On the vertical axis is a measure of work-induced happiness which is the happiness we feel as a result of being able to spend the income we derive from work (but not the happiness we derive from other sources or that might be inherent in our psychological makeup). It is assumed that the rate of remuneration per hour remains constant. The vertical axis also measures the work-induced unhappiness we experience because work is, on balance, unpleasant.

The heavy solid line in the upper graph indicates the work-induced *happiness* we feel as the number of hours we work per week increases. Note that as the number of hours increases so does our weekly income and our work-induced happiness. But note that the increase in happiness gets smaller and smaller as our income (hours per week) increases. The idea behind these smaller and smaller increases is that as our income rises we find less urgent ways to spend our income. Thus the first $100 per week you earn might be spent on essentials like food and power while the last $100 is spent on luxuries like a restaurant meal or a massage.

The light solid line in the upper graph shows the work-induced *unhappiness* we experience as the number of hours we work per week increases. As the number of hours of work increases so does the total unhappiness we experience. But note that the increase in unhappiness becomes larger and larger as the number of hours we work per week increases. To understand why, consider how much unpleasantness the second hour of work in a day yields as compared to an extra hour of work on top of your normal working day. It is easy to see that the extra hour after you have been working for some hours comes at a greater cost to you than does the extra hour when you haven't been working long.

Recall that in the upper graph the heavy, solid line shows total-happiness-from-work (from the income derived from work) at each possible number of hours of work per week while the light, solid line shows the total-unhappiness-from-work at each possible number of hours per week. Given these two curves, how many hours per week will the happiness-maximizing person work? The answer is that she will choose that level of work for which the excess of happiness over unhappiness is greatest. This is shown as A hours in the graph where the vertical distance between the two curves is greatest. To see why this maximizes happiness, consider a lower number of hours per week. At a lower number of hours the vertical difference between the happiness line and the unhappiness line is smaller than it was at A. The net level of happiness is lower to the left of A than it is at A. Now consider a larger number of hours per week. You can see that the vertical difference between the happiness line and the unhappiness line is smaller than at point A.

The light, solid total-unhappiness-from-work line drawn on the upper graph assumes that there are no negative externalities – that there is no basis for the fundamental flaw in the system that causes excessive work effort, excessive consumption and excessive environmental degradation and congestion all of which lower our QOL. If we now imagine that all workers were to take into account the fact that each hour of work they undertake results in negative externalities like pollution and congestion, then the unhappiness they derive from work would be much higher at each possible number of hours worked per week. Taking this increased unhappiness into account we can derive a total-unhappiness-from-work line which includes the unhappiness caused by these negative externalities. This is shown as the broken curve in the upper graph. Note that it lies above the light, solid total-unhappiness-from-work line that does not include the unhappiness caused by negative externalities. (In this analysis we are assuming that positive externalities are negligible but, if we wished to be precise, we would describe this broken curve as reflecting the excess of the cost of negative externalities over the much smaller benefits of the positive externalities.)

If we now compare the heavy, solid total-happiness-from-work line with the broken total-unhappiness-from-work line it can be seen that the number of hours of work per week that maximizes the excess of happiness over unhappiness (including negative externalities) is now at point B which involves fewer hours of work per week than at point A. Note also that if we continue to work the number of hours per week indicated by point A, the excess of happiness over unhappiness is lower than it would be at point B. These relationships can be confirmed by looking at the curves in the lower graph.

In the lower graph, the vertical axis now shows net happiness which is the excess of happiness over unhappiness; the horizontal axis continues to show hours worked per week. The solid curve in this graph shows what the excess of happiness over unhappiness would be for each level of hours worked if there were no negative externalities; its vertical height corresponds to the vertical distance between the heavy, solid line and the light, solid line in the upper diagram. It can be seen that it reaches a maximum at A hours. This solid curve in the lower graph is the one that guides the individual's work − leisure decision when the negative externalities associated with work are not taken into account.

The broken curve in the lower graph shows the excess of happiness over unhappiness when negative externalities are taken into account. Its height corresponds to the vertical distance between the heavy, solid line and the broken line in the upper graph. Because the negative externalities are now taken into account, this curve lies wholly below the solid curve; the excess of happiness over unhappiness − net happiness − is smaller for every level of hours worked. Furthermore, you can see that this broken curve reaches a maximum at B which corresponds to a lower number of hours per week than at point A. Note also that once we acknowledge that production and consumption of goods and services results in more negative externalities than positive externalities as a matter of course, the solid net happiness from work line should no longer have practical relevance for the happiness-maximizing worker as it does not reflect the true net happiness gained by an individual from the work effort they undertake.

You can see in the upper graph that at point B there is still a level of unhappiness caused by negative externalities (measured by the vertical distance between the light, solid line and the broken line). The reduction in work hours has reduced the negative externalities but not eliminated them. This level of negative externalities is the level that is consistent with maximization of well-being *given that we now take these external costs into account.*[8]

SO WHY DON'T WE REDUCE OUR WORK HOURS?

We have established that taking account of the effect of our work effort on environmental disamenity would cause us to maximize our happiness by working fewer hours per week. But, the reality is that we don't take these negative externalities into account. We compare the dollar income we receive from undertaking unpleasant work with the consumer goods and services it enables us to buy. We neglect entirely the fact that the work we undertake in order to earn income, and the consumption this income allows, both have unpleasant environmental effects.

Furthermore, even if we were fully aware of the environmental disamentity that our work effort causes, we would not rationally choose to reduce our work effort. To see why, imagine that, because you are aware of these negative externalities you decrease your work effort while everyone else, unaware of the full cost of the environmental disamenity they cause, continues to work long hours. When you work fewer hours you make no significant difference to the total environmental disamenity that exists in the economy. You have reduced the negative externalities that you impose on others but they have not done the same for you. You are working fewer hours but the environment is just as polluted and there is just as much traffic congestion; so why not continue to work longer hours like everyone else? You are still on that forced ride to somewhere you don't want to go. Outcomes like this are sometimes described by economists as the result of a 'tyranny of the majority' or, as Fred Hirsch described them, the 'tyranny of small decisions'.[9]

The degree to which individuals are forced to ride to an undesirable destination also has an international dimension. Thus, to the extent that developed countries face lower levels of domestic environmental disamenity because many environmentally damaging industrial activities are carried out in developing countries, it is the citizens of these developing countries who are most exposed to the costs of forced riding. This issue is taken up again in Chapter 7.

At this stage, the reader might be wondering why, if *individuals* have nothing to gain from reducing their work hours, there has not been agitation to have these hours reduced in a *collective* way through changed legislative arrangements or through work place bargaining. As we shall see in Chapter 7, which deals with policy responses to the fundamental flaw, countries with a more centralized approach to the issue of work hours have actually had greater success in reducing hours. However, even in these cases, it appears that issues such as child-raising or family commitments are the motivation for seeking shorter hours rather than the pervasiveness of negative externalities. Thus, even when collective outcomes are considered, we find that because of ignorance of the fundamental flaw, we are working many more hours than would maximize our happiness.

As will be seen in Chapter 5, this is evidenced by the documented decline in well-being that has occurred in both the US and Europe over the past 30 years or more − a decline in well-being that has occurred in spite of very large increases in GDP per capita over this same period. However, we shall see later in this chapter that declines in aggregate work time in Europe as compared to the US suggest that the extent to which European workers are short-changed by negative externalities is lower than in the case of US workers.

SOME REFINEMENT OF THE ARGUMENT

It was earlier explained that the graphical model presented here is for the typical or representative individual. In reality, there will be a range of outcomes for different individuals. Some will have high work-related incomes per hour from which they derive high levels of happiness for any given number of hours worked; others will have low incomes per hour from which lower levels of happiness are derived. As we saw in Chapter 2, the extent of unhappiness derived from a given amount work will also vary across occupations. Depending on such diverse factors as age, gender, marital status, occupation and place of residence, the negative externalities experienced by each individual are also likely to vary to a greater or lesser degree. Although it would only muddy the waters to look at the implications of all possible differences between individuals, there are two differences that will assist our understanding of the notion of the fundamental flaw and its implications.

One of these is differences in income per hour; the other is differences in the level of negative externalities experienced by different individuals. At this stage we look only at differences in income per hour. Later, in Chapter 6, we shall also look at the effects of differences in the level of negative externalities experienced by individuals in different countries – especially the differences between individuals who live in countries that are heavily involved in 'dirty' manufacturing as compared to those who dwell in countries that are more reliant on 'clean' service industries. In that context it will also be found to be fruitful to look the extent to which such differences occur between developed and developing countries.

In order to understand clearly the relevance of differences in income per hour, it is convenient to assume, for purposes of explication, that the negative externalities generated within a country are pervasive and that all individuals in society are subject to a similar level of costs associated with them.[10] If, in this case, the range of incomes per hour that individuals earn varies significantly, it will be found that low-income earners suffer negative externality costs that are a larger proportion of their incomes than would high-income earners. This means that, in acknowledging the fundamental flaw, low-income earners should reduce work hours by more than high-income earners. While such an outcome would optimize work effort it would, unfortunately, aggravate income inequality. Indeed, such an effect would reinforce the existing tendency for the distribution of income to be widened because some workers, such as those in professional occupations, work longer hours than do other workers. As was pointed out in Chapter 2, these workers tend to work longer hours because they dislike their work less (enjoy it more) than do other workers. Not only is the degree of income inequality widened because professional workers earn higher incomes per hour than most other workers but the tendency for them to work longer hours also has the same effect. Furthermore, as environmental and development economist James K. Boyce has demonstrated, increased inequality tends to 'raise the valuation of benefits reaped by rich and powerful winners, relative to costs imposed on poor and less powerful losers.'[11] The upshot of this change in relative valuations is for the overall level of environmental degradation to increase. In terms of the analysis undertaken here, this suggests that low-income earners may be in a double bind: if, in taking account of the fundamental flaw, they reduce their work hours by more than the rich, the environmental gains accruing from this decreased work effort may be offset by the reduced environmental amenity that accompanies the subsequent increase in income inequality.

Notwithstanding these complex ramifications of income inequality, throughout this book we shall put aside the issue of the effect of negative externalities on workers with different incomes so that we can emphasize the situation of the typical or representative worker in an endeavour to see by how much their work time should be reduced as a result of a new found cognizance of the fundamental flaw. As noted above we shall, however, discuss some income-based differences between workers in high-income countries and those in low-income countries later in Chapter 6. In the next section we see how changing perceptions of the cost of environmental disamenity can negate the claimed benefits of increases in GDP per capita.

PERCEPTIONS OF THE COSTS OF ENVIRONMENTAL DISAMENITY

We have noted above, and will explain in detail in Chapter 5, that developed countries have experienced a noticeable decline in well-being over the last 30 years or more *in spite of very large increases in GDP per capita.* It is a widely accepted tenet of the environmental economics literature that, like leisure, environmental amenity is, in the terminology introduced in the previous chapter, a luxury that we desire more of as our GDP per capita rises. This means that as GDP per capita rises, a given physical level of environmental amenity can be expected to become more valuable to society. Put another way, as our GDP per capita increases, a given physical level of environmental disamenity is perceived to cost us more. This is clearly evidenced by society's historically increasing concern for the environment as GDP per capita has grown. Thus, even without the increased environmental degradation that has occurred over the past 30 years or more, it would not have been possible for well-being to have risen at the rate suggested by the rate of increase in GDP per capita. The upshot of this is that there is the potential for the work, leisure trade-off to become further and further removed from the optimum as, over time, GDP per capita increases, *even if environmental degradation does not worsen.*

The reality is, of course, that the situation is more serious than this. Over time, GDP per capita has risen while degradation of the environment has actually become worse. Over time, each dollar spent on material goods buys (unintentionally) environmental degradation that has a higher and higher cost in relation to the value of the goods and services that caused this degradation.

Advocates of economic growth may dispute this reasoning, arguing that consciousness of the potential environmental problems we might face has reduced the level of environmental disamenity in many countries in recent years. Although the validity of this reasoning is highly questionable, the important thing to understand is that regardless of whether or not we have become more environmentally responsible in recent times, the relevant question is not whether current levels of environmental disamenity are greater or less than they were previously but, rather, are the current levels of work, consumption and environmental disamenity in excess of what would maximize our well-being? It is not a matter of whether we are doing better than in the past – although this may be useful information to have – but how well we are doing in relation to what is optimal.

In making comparisons with the past rather than looking for what is optimal, we are conforming to the precepts of prospect theory that explains a human tendency to emphasise *changes* in variables rather than their *absolute values.* This tendency results from a greater accessibility of information about the former as compared to the latter.[12] Thus it is very hard for us to compare the current state of the world with an alternative state in which we might work less and consume less but have a cleaner environment. We have demonstrated, using economic theory, that current levels of work and consumption are in excess of those required to maximize our individual welfare; it follows that we would be better off if we worked less, consumed less and damaged the environment less. Unfortunately, however, as we shall see in the next chapter, there are powerful forces at work in the economy that tend to encourage rather than discourage consumption and the environmental degradation it causes.

THE ENVIRONMENTAL PAY-OFF FROM LESS WORK

All other factors remaining constant, less work means less total output. Empirical evidence of the extent to which less work equals less output can be found in the work of American economist Robert Gordon who has undertaken an analysis of data that indicates the relative performances of the economies of the US and Europe over the past two centuries. As an economist who understands the limitations of his own discipline, he says in his study, 'looking back at the long history of Europe falling behind the US and then catching up, it is hard to avoid the conclusion that this topic has more to do with politics and history than with economics.'[13] In relation to the effect of work hours on the relative performance of the US and European economies, Gordon notes that '[t]o the extent that Europe's standard of living (measured by its relative output per capita) is held down by lower hours due to longer vacations, then its citizens have chosen to use some of their prosperity to take longer vacations in contrast to overworked Americans.'[14] (He may well have added that the citizens of Europe have used some of their prosperity to increase social and environmental amenity. Indeed, economist Richard Layard asks whether the fact that since 1975 happiness has stagnated in the US but risen in Europe can be explained by superior work-life balance in Europe.[15]) In looking at the effect of work effort on output it can be seen that this comparison of output in Europe with that of the US has some similarities to a comparison of the West German part of reunified Germany with the Eastern part where, in order to protect annual output per worker, work hours have remained significantly higher since reunification.[16]

Juliet Schor provides this simple justification for the link between economic output and environmental degradation:

> Although choice of technology and product, as well as numerous other factors, are
> key determinants of the extent of environmental degradation, it is difficult to deny

the role of growth itself. More production of steel and autos creates more air pollution and global warming, more newspapers and houses lead to the felling of more trees, more food generally implies more pesticides, and increased output in the petrochemical industry is accompanied by a rise in toxic substances.[17]

A useful construct for understanding the importance of lower output for environmental amenity is the IPAT model. In this model, environmental impact (I) is the result of population (P), per capita GDP or affluence (A), and technology (T). It is easy to see that if population and technology are held constant, the environmental impact increases with GDP per capita. Of course, if GDP per capita increases with increasing work hours, environmental impact can be expected to increase with increased work hours. The common riposte to the gloomy prognosis contained in this model is that technological change will more than compensate for any rise in GDP per capita – leading to a reduction in environmental impact. This is a very contentious area which is characterized by disputes between optimists, who argue that technology can indeed deliver the cleaner environment that is increasingly demanded as affluence increases, and pessimists who point out that increases in environmental amenity in pockets of developed countries have, as their counterpart, increased environmental disamenity in developing countries which have become offshore havens for the developed countries' dirty activities. The end result, say the pessimists, is an aggregate worsening of the global environment. If the pessimists are correct, there is little more that needs to be said – lower levels of economic activity accompanying shorter hours will reduce environmental disamenity. If, on the other hand, the optimists are correct, which seems doubtful, then shorter work hours will complement the beneficial effects of technology, giving an even greater improvement in the environment. In either case, recognition of the fundamental flaw and the need for reduced work hours to optimize the trade-off between work and leisure will result in lower levels of environmental damage and increased well-being.

So why is it doubtful that the optimists are correct? The major evidence put forward by the optimists is that in developed countries, environmental disamenity (often measured by levels of pollution) per dollar of GDP (national output) has been declining over recent decades. This contrasts with the increasing environmental disamenity per dollar of GDP that has been experienced by many rapidly growing developing countries over the same period. The optimists thus hypothesize that increasing environmental disamenity occurs up to some threshold level of GDP after which it declines.[18]

The fact that environmental disamenity has been growing at a slower rate than GDP in developed countries may, at first blush, seem to be incontrovertible evidence of the power of increasing affluence to diminish environmental disamenity. However, even if we neglect the fact that much environmentally harmful production has been moved offshore from developed countries, there is a gross methodological defect in this analysis. Later, in Chapter 5, when the shortcomings of GDP as a measure of well-being are discussed, it will be shown that in spite of large increases in GDP per capita in the US since the mid-1970s, quality of life has actually fallen. But how can quality of life fall if much more output (GDP) is being produced today as compared to 30 years ago? One of the reasons is that much of this output is being directed at solving the problems that are caused by pollution, resource depletion and congestion. This increased output does not increase our well-being − it is simply defensive expenditure that aims to correct the adverse effects of economic activity.

The optimists are neglecting the feedback loop that manifests itself in a tendency for growth in GDP (national output) to be increasingly devoted to reducing the ill-effects of otherwise beneficial economic activity. As resources are increasingly used to maintain yields from depleted fisheries, ward off the effects of global warming, and clean up pollution and toxic waste, there is a decline in the proportion of GDP that actually raises well-being − as opposed to preventing it from falling. So the optimists make the mistake of comparing levels of environmental disamenity with total GDP rather than with that part of GDP that is actually raising well-being; that is, GDP net of the defensive expenditures. If, in the US over the past 30 years, environmental disamenity has been rising at a faster rate than GDP net of defensive expenditures, the optimist's position is untenable. If a significant part of the increases in GDP that have occurred over the past 30 years or so have had the purpose of reducing environmental disamenity as well as ameliorating other negative effects of GDP growth such as congestion, then it might well have been better to have never reached such high levels of GDP in the first place. Rather than fouling the nest and having to use more and more resources to clean it out, it may have been better not to have fouled it in the first place.

It is clear that fewer hours worked will, all other factors remaining constant, result in less output per capita which results in less environmental disamenity caused by production and consumption of goods and services. Make no mistake, when bricklayers work fewer hours they lay fewer bricks, when chefs spend fewer days at work they cook fewer meals and when truck drivers drive for fewer hours fewer goods are delivered.

The most important tenet of the environmental movement is, perhaps, the almost universally accepted argument that population growth must be curbed to save the planet. It is easy to deduce from the IPAT model that for a given population, a reduction in work hours will have a similar effect to a reduction in population. So long as world income is above subsistence level, the reduction in production and consumption resulting from a decrease in hours worked is likely to be roughly similar to the reduction in production and consumption brought about by a reduction in population of similar proportion.

Regardless of the precise effect that a future regime of shorter hours would have on the environment, there is clear evidence that shorter working hours can be accompanied by far lower levels of environmental degradation than are currently attributable to economic activity in the US. The evidence can be found in a comparison of the environmental degradation per capita caused by hard working American citizens with that of the citizens of Europe where both the hours worked per employee and the ratio of employees to total population have fallen to such an extent in the past 30 years that they are now exceeded by those in the US by something approaching 20 per cent.[19] Our comparison is aided by looking at the ecological footprints for the US and some selected European countries.

Recall that in Chapter 2 we saw that a country's ecological footprint is the per capita call that each nation makes on the global environment. It measures the use of environmental resources attributable to each country no matter whether or not the resources used are located in the country itself. In 2000, the ecological footprint for the US was over 400 per cent of the world average.[20] For a selected group of European nations for which we have data on hours worked and participation rates, the (weighted) average ecological footprint was approximately 200 per cent of the world average. Thus the ecological footprint (per capita) of the US is approximately twice that of these European countries although hours worked per capita in the US are less than 50 per cent higher.[21] The European experience attests to the fact that a given reduction in working hours *can be* accompanied by a more than proportional reduction in environmental degradation. When we look, in Chapter 6, at the cumulative effect of the fundamental flaw over the past century we shall see that there is also the potential, over the long course of history, for a compounding of the environmentally beneficial effect of shorter work hours.

Rather than point to the fundamental flaw as the basis for excessive work hours and excessive consumption, many commentators, including some economists, argue that these problems are caused by an inappropriate desire to keep up with the Joneses. These claims are tested in the next chapter. The last word is given to Barbara Ward and René Dubos authors of *Only One Earth*.

Do we confront yet another 'treadmill' situation – more economic growth needed to provide the resources to clear up the mess made by economic growth and in the process creating still more economic mess to be cleared up?[22]

NOTES

1   Mishan, E.J. (1969), *The Costs of Economic Growth*, Harmondsworth: Pelican, p. 154*f.*
2   OECD (1989), *Economic Instruments for Environmental Protection*, Paris: OECD.

3   Durning, A.T. (2002), 'How Much is "Enough"?', Chap. 5.8 in Broad, R. (2002), *Global Backlash*, Lanham MD: Rowman and Littlefield, p. 288.
4   Princen, T., Maniates, M. and Conca, K. (2002), 'Confronting Consumption', Chap. 1 in Princen, T., Maniates, M. and Conca, K., *Confronting Consumption*, Cambridge, MA: MIT Press, p. 16.
5   Princen, T. (2002), 'Distancing: Consumption and the Severing of Feedback', Chap. 5 in Princen et al., *Confronting Consumption*, Cambridge, MA: MIT Press, p. 116.
6   Hirsch, F. (1977), *The Social Limits to Growth*, London: Routledge & Keegan Paul, p. 91*n*.
7   Putnam, R.D. (2000), *Bowling Alone*, New York: Simon & Schuster, p. 406.
8   For ease of exposition it has been assumed in these graphs that the costs of negative externalities result only in an upward shift of the unhappiness-from-work curve. Although it does not change the argument, it might be more realistic to have these negative externalities both raise the total-unhappiness-from-work curve and lower the total-happiness-from-work curve because some negative externalities affect the pleasure we get from consumption expenditure.
9   See Hirsch (1977). As is discussed in Chapter 4, game theory, in particular the prisoner's dilemma, has also been productively applied to these situations.
10   This assumption requires that the increasing preference for a clean environment as income rises (discussed in the next section) is a function of aggregate national income rather than the income of individuals within a nation.
11   Boyce, James K. (2002), *The Political Economy of the Environment*, Cheltenham, UK and Northampton, MA, USA: Edward Elgar, p. 41.
12   See Kahneman, Daniel (2002), 'Maps of Bounded Rationality: a Perspective on Intuitive Judgement and Choice', Nobel Prize Lecture, especially pp. 481–82.
13   Gordon, R.J. (2002). 'Two Centuries of Economic Growth: Europe Chasing the American Frontier', Economic History Workshop, Northwestern University, October, p. 38.
14   Ibid., p. 9.
15   See Layard, Richard (2005), *Happiness*, New York: Penguin, pp. 50–51.
16   See Witte, J.M. (2002), 'The Last Gasps of "Model Germany"', Washington: American Institute for Contemporary German Studies, at http://www.aicgs.org/c/wittec.shtml, accessed 18 December 2003.
17   Schor, Juliet (1991), 'Global Equity and Environmental Crisis: An Argument for Reducing Working Hours in the North', *World Development*, **19** (1), p. 75.
18   The graphical shape of this relationship is often rather awkwardly described as the Environmental Kuznets Curve. The reason for the name need not detain us here. It is argued that, in general, developing countries have not yet reached this threshold whereas developed countries have passed it.
19   See Gordon (2002), especially p. 8, notes 9 and 10.
20   Because the world average includes the US, the footprint of the US will be more than 400 per cent of that of the rest of the world.
21   The figure would be 44 per cent if both the participation rate and hours worked per worker were both 20 per cent higher in the US than in Europe. See Ibid.
22   Ward, B. and Dubos, R. (1972), *Only one Earth*, Harmondsworth: Penguin, p. 198.

4. Critiques of Consumerism and the Consumption Treadmill

With the exception of the instinct of self-preservation, the propensity for emulation is probably the strongest and most alert and persistent of the economic motives.[1]

Thorstein Veblen

There is a very significant body of literature in which it is argued that a major shortcoming of contemporary society is its excessive emphasis on consumption. But why is there so much concern that current levels of consumption are excessive? At the grass roots level this stems from the feeling that in spite of rising incomes and rising levels of consumption, people seem no happier than in the past. From a social science perspective, there is corroborating evidence for this view. It is found in the growing body of research into the level and causes of human happiness. As we shall see in the next chapter, this research suggests that our gut feelings are correct – rising incomes and consumption have not raised happiness in the recent past. This means that significant sacrifices of environmental amenity are being made without any corresponding increase in human welfare. As we have already demonstrated, this rising tide of consumerism is due, at least in part, to the fact that we are all being duped into working and consuming more as a result of a fundamental flaw in the system. This fundamental flaw prevents us from achieving work-life balance because it prevents us from voluntarily choosing to devote more time to leisure and less to work. In this chapter we look at the way in which emulation of our peers can exacerbate the problems created by the fundamental flaw. We do so by looking at the liberal economic approach to consumerism in the context of more pervasive critiques.

CRITIQUES OF CONSUMER SOCIETY

Critiques of material consumption are nothing new. Francis Fukuyama, in making his case for capitalist liberal democracy as the ultimate stage in the evolution of society, argues that such a position is not threatened by antagonists of progress. In doing so, he points to the 18th-century philosopher, Rousseau, as the founder of the idea that 'what could potentially make man happy... would be to get off the treadmill of modern technology and the endless cycle of wants it creates, and to recover some of the wholeness of natural man'.[2] Using evidence from the 18th and 19th centuries, economist Albert Hirschman argues that critiques of material consumption are a typical response to periods of economic expansion when growth in the quantity and range of consumer goods available brings benefits to a broader cross section of society.[3]

A common theme in the numerous critiques of consumer society that come from contemporary commentators such as philosophers, psychologists, sociologists, political scientists and a small band of economists is the idea that we are consuming too much for our own good – or, at least, consuming too much of the wrong things for our own good. Most of these arguments are seen as elitist by liberal economists. Juliet Schor, although critical of the liberal approach, succinctly sums up its advantages. 'The liberal approach to consumption combines a deep respect for the consumer's ability to act in her own best interest and an emphasis on the efficiency gains of unregulated consumer markets: a commitment to liberty and the general welfare.'[4]

The most commonly encountered critiques of consumerism include one or more of the following ideas:[5]

- some critics of consumerism argue that we can't think for ourselves and are thus subject to the greed-induced persuasion of capitalists that is manifested in marketing and advertising;
- some argue that we don't act as individuals but follow a herd mentality requiring us to consume whatever the tribe is consuming;
- in an interesting twist, others argue that our desire to be different from the mainstream means that we must continually seek consumption patterns that set us apart.

From the liberal economic perspective, these arguments are seen as elitist in that they generally deny that individuals are the best judges of their own welfare. Some elitist critiques attack the volume of consumption engaged in by individuals. The calls to limit advertising, to discourage consumption by taxing consumer goods, to encourage saving, or to encourage a more contemplative lifestyle are all attacks on the liberty of individuals that come from commentators who claim to be better judges of welfare than the individuals themselves. (From this group of commentators, we should exclude the many committed environmentalists – sometimes described as members of the voluntary simplicity movement – who practise what they preach and who, without necessarily realizing it, are attempting to promote a sustainable society by encouraging behaviour that compensates for the fundamental flaw that is central to the problem of overwork and over consumption.)

Other elitist critiques are centred around the issue of taste. What many commentators object to is not the volume of consumption but its composition. Put simply, academics and intellectuals who eat at small cafés, collect antiques, spend much of their leisure time reading or attending art galleries or the theatre would, for reasons best known to themselves, prefer to see their fellow human beings do likewise rather than see them eating fast food, purchasing consumer durables, and playing computer games or attending blockbuster movies. Again, the view is that the elite knows best what is good for the masses. Gary Cross, commenting on the ideological clash between intellectuals and the masses during the first half of the 20th century, argues that '[c]oncern about the unleashed mass libido was never distinguishable from merely the intellectual's ascetic dislike of the libertine taste of the masses; and attacks on mass-market play were often little more than a barely disguised resentment of the wage-earner's growing consumer sovereignty.'[6] For economists, refutation of these critiques is simply a matter of the defence of individual liberty. As Nobel Prize winner Robert Solow has put it. 'The attack on consumer sovereignty performs the same function as the doctrine of "repressive tolerance". If people do not want what I see so clearly they should want, it can only be that they don't know what they "really" want.'[7]

From a liberal economic perspective there are, however, two possible caveats to this charge of elitism levelled at the critics of consumerism. One is concerned with market failure in the form of information asymmetry. We return to it later in this chapter. The other is concerned with the desire to emulate our peers. It is sometimes said that this desire subjects us to life on a treadmill where, in spite of our efforts, our increased consumption leaves us standing still.

THE CONSUMPTION TREADMILL

Although most critiques of consumer society are deemed to be elitist and inconsistent with the assumption that consumers are the best judges of their own welfare, the consumption treadmill argument is held by some mainstream economists to fit squarely within the liberal tradition.[8] Like the argument that underpins the explanation of the fundamental flaw, this argument also involves the idea of market failure in the form of negative externalities.

It is a basic assumption of economic theory that goods and services are purchased solely for the satisfaction that they convey to the purchaser who is unconcerned with the consumption behaviour of others.[9] (Consumers are assumed to make no interpersonal comparisons of the happiness derived from consumption.) If, on the contrary, goods and services are purchased to a greater or lesser degree simply because they are purchased by other consumers, then, a market failure can occur. In the language we have developed in the previous chapters, if, when our neighbour buys a new car, an overseas holiday or some extra years schooling for their children, we feel compelled to do likewise we experience a negative consumption externality.

That is, the act of purchase by our neighbour confers an external cost on us although we were not a party to the transaction that resulted in this purchase. The point is that if our neighbour had not undertaken this consumption neither would we. Consumption expenditure motivated by a desire to keep up with the Joneses is thus construed as leading to a loss of well-being. Economists who have specialized in an analysis of this emulative behaviour have argued that in certain circumstances it does in fact reduce well-being while in others it does not.

Fred Hirsch, in one of the most influential economic treatments of the ills of contemporary society, undertook much of the modern analytical work devoted to the economic effects of emulative behaviour.[10] He coined the term 'positional goods' for those goods and services that have the strong characteristic of demonstrating the economic status of the person who acquires them. He had in mind the idea that although increased income can provide all members of society with more of some material goods such as food, clothing and household durables, rising income cannot make some possessions such as the house on the hill or a painting by the late Jackson Pollock more abundant. Thus economic growth has a tendency to fail to deliver because increasing affluence fails to facilitate the purchase of these positional goods. As Gary Cross has put it:

> Mass affluence placed environmental limits on personal enjoyment (crowded highways on Sundays, for example) and reduced the value of status goods which declined in proportion to the degree that others had acquired them.[11]

Hirsch was careful to point out that in the case of some positional goods, where no additional social resources are used to attempt to achieve ownership, the social costs of this 'positionality' may be low or even zero. (The house on the hill or the Jackson Pollock painting are good examples of these positional goods because they are in fixed supply and the increased purchase price that goes with the increased affluence of the potential buyers means that a transfer is simply made from the new owner to the current owner.) On the other hand, when competition between individuals for acquisition of positional goods involves the use of additional resources to produce more of them, there is a waste of society's resources. A favourite example of this waste is credentialism in education where people attain ever higher academic qualifications in order to be better placed to gain employment – only to find that their competitors have done likewise with the result that their likelihood of gaining the desired job has not changed. Unfortunately, real resources – including the students' time – have been dissipated in raising the qualifications of all to no advantage. These resources could have been deployed elsewhere or not expended at all.

In the context of the basic argument being put forward here, the important point to note is that these consumers of education have undertaken consumption that has made no difference to their happiness – indeed, if the education was time-consuming and painful, their happiness may have been diminished. (This example supposes that the education in question has the sole function of screening applicants for jobs and does not in any way raise their inherent work place productivity. Researchers aver that sometimes this is the case and sometimes it is not.[12])

EXTENSIONS OF HIRSCH'S ANALYSIS

Recent contributions to the economic literature dealing with positional goods have extended Hirsch's analysis to a wide range of goods and services that he had not considered. As we noted above, it can be argued that purchases as straightforward as the new car, fridge, running shoes or the annual vacation to a particular destination can have a strong positional component – we acquire them to be one step ahead of our neighbour, only to find that our neighbour who now suffers the negative externality from our consumption feels compelled to acquire them as well. This, in turn, confers a negative externality on us, leaving us in the same relative position as before – unable to feel smug about our superiority over our fellow human beings.

The idea that our neighbour's consumption of positional goods can have adverse effects on our well-being has some similarities with the idea that when our neighbour strikes misfortune this also has adverse affects on our well-being. In all liberal democracies governments are moved to require individuals to protect themselves against serious harm. Whether it is motorcycle riders who are required to wear a helmet, smokers who are urged to quit, or recreational sailors who are required to carry safety equipment, society overrides their individual liberty in an endeavour to limit the harm they may experience as a result of their voluntary actions. The reason that individual liberty is overridden in these cases is not only because we feel sorry for those who are harmed but also because we feel duty bound to assist, at our own cost, with treatment for the harm. They subject us to what economists call a caring externality. The helmet, the quit campaign and the safety gear are all made compulsory because, in the event of the individual coming to serious harm, the state, and ultimately the taxpayer, will pick up the tab for the treatment. When our neighbours strike misfortune they impose on us an external cost – the compulsion to assist them – which can be reduced if individual liberty is curtailed. Just as we mandate safe behaviour in an endeavour to minimize the externalities imposed on us by neighbours who may get into trouble, so a case can be made for minimizing the adverse effect of excessive consumption by discouraging the consumption of positional goods. Although a policy of restricting the consumption of positional goods is not a likely development in liberal democratic societies, an alternative policy – that of reducing the capacity for consumption by mandating shorter work hours – is already a common feature of modern economies. This is an issue that we return to when we examine policy options in Chapter 7.

Another way in which the effects of the treadmill may be exacerbated in affluent societies is through what sociologists describe as the Diderot effect. Based on Enlightenment philosopher Diderot's need to replace shabby items in his study as a result of the receipt of a gift of a new red dressing gown, this effect describes the need to replace a range of old, related possessions as a result of acquisition of a single new possession.[13] Whether or not it is the consumption treadmill that leads us to replace those running shoes or the fridge, their replacement might result in the consequent acquisition of a complete new running outfit or a new set of kitchen appliances.

In an interesting twist to the theory of positional goods, Joseph Heath has used the work of Thomas Frank to show that the costs of this consumption treadmill may be even more entrenched in capitalist societies than formerly supposed.[14] This is because contemporary consumerism is said to be characterized by rebellion against whatever is popular. It is neither cool nor hip to be consuming in the same way as others. Consumers are thus driven to find ever new patterns of consumption – patterns that quickly become obsolete when those who are uncool attempt to remedy the situation by adopting them. Rather than us wanting to emulate our neighbour by trading up to a superior fridge like theirs, we want an entirely different fridge. Once we acquire it we are briefly satisfied until such time as the neighbour acquires one and it loses its (metaphoric) cool. Then we must look again for the cool, as yet undiscovered, alternative. In many instances we are the victims of a double whammy. When a new product such as the cell phone or a new fashion accessory is introduced we get on the treadmill trying to emulate our neighbours who bought one first. Soon, however, the conformity gets to us and we are compelled to buy the different version that will set us apart from the run of the mill.

Whether we are driven to emulate our neighbours or to be different from them, the effect is the same: we are forever on the consumption treadmill acquiring new consumption goods and services on the basis of the behaviour of our neighbours. Unfortunately, taking exercise on this treadmill compromises work-life balance because it involves working longer hours and using more of society's scarce resources – resources that include environmental assets such as clean air, fisheries, forests and open space.

The consumption treadmill, no matter how distasteful it is to critics of consumerism, has been an integral part of capitalism since its inception. In his *Theory of the Leisure Class* published in 1899 Thorstein Veblen, who is classed as an institutional economist and certainly not in the mainstream, commented that '... no general increase of the community's wealth can make any approach to satiating this need [for wealth], the ground of which is the desire for every one to excel every one else in the accumulation of goods.'[15]

Although most prominent among the middle and upper classes during the industrial revolution, in recent times, with the enormous growth in discretionary income, this tendency has become pervasive across virtually all strata of society. In fact, positional competition in sport, in personal beauty, and in the arts has to a greater or lesser degree characterized communities since ancient times. It has even been argued that if survival of our ancestors was enhanced by being of high status, the desire for status and its trappings may be built into our genes.[16] Many of the academics who are critical of our willingness to stay on the consumption treadmill may themselves be engaging in positional competition on a publication treadmill where they compete with their peers for academic recognition and promotion. As Richard Easterlin, a pioneer of studies into the determinants of happiness, has put it: 'to scholars vitally concerned with professional reputation in a competitive field of learning, it should hardly come as a surprise that relative status is an important ingredient of happiness.'[17]

WHY DON'T WE STEP OFF THE TREADMILL?

An ultra liberal critique of the hypothesis that pursuit of positional goods reduces our well-being might be that individuals are free to step off the consumption treadmill at any time. If keeping up with the Joneses (or making sure we're different from them) reduces our welfare then why don't we simply decide not to continue to engage in the competition?

One explanation might be that we are faced with what game theorists describe as a prisoner's dilemma. In the context of status-seeking consumption, this involves members of society being faced with a situation in which no one is likely to move away from the status quo (involving widespread consumption of positional goods) because a unilateral decision by an individual to make such a move would reduce their happiness.[18] This can be explained by considering the matrix in Figure 4.1 which, in representing society as consisting of just two consumers, provides a simple model that can, nonetheless, be extrapolated to the more complex society of reality. In Figure 4.1 contemporary capitalist society is characterized by the lower right cell which represents the situation where both consumers choose to consume a given status-conferring positional good (or service). The outcome is the same for both consumers and is clearly more likely to occur than the situations where one consumer chooses not to consume the good. This is because in these situations the happiness of one consumer is diminished in relation to the other. However, if both consumers could agree not to consume the status-conferring positional good, they would end up in the upper left cell where the savings from not consuming the good could be used to purchase other goods or services or allow an increase in leisure time. Those commentators who consider that the pursuit of status through consumption is undesirable would like to see society move from its current position in the lower right cell to the upper left cell. Being aware that individuals are unlikely to go it alone and reduce their consumption of the status-enhancing good (and risk the likelihood that other consumers do not follow suit) these commentators would see a role for the state in promoting

CONSUMER 1

	Doesn't Consume	Does Consume
CONSUMER 2 — Doesn't Consume	Consumers have equivalent happiness and well-being is maximized	Consumer 1 feels superior Consumer 2 feels Inferior
CONSUMER 2 — Does Consume	Consumer 2 feels superior Consumer 1 feels inferior	Consumers have equivalent happiness but well-being is not maximized

Figure 4.1 Outcomes from consumer choices

behaviour modification designed to force all consumers into the upper left cell. Nevertheless, the tradition in mainstream economics is that it is a discipline that describes rather than prescribes people's behaviour. This being the case, contemporary economists who advocate state intervention to reduce the effects of emulative behaviour are going against that tradition.

A second explanation as to why individuals do not step off the consumption treadmill is concerned with the economist's notion of bounded rationality − the inability to compute what is objectively in our best interest in a highly complex world. Kaufman describes bounded rationality as a state in which '...behaviour is purposeful but less than optimal due to human cognitive limitations.'[19] Is the problem that these cognitive limitations mean that we are unable to see that stepping off the treadmill is in our best interests? If so, can we learn from the behaviour of older citizens whose limited life expectancy may allow them to overcome these cognitive limitations? As academic and judge, Richard Posner, points out 'the old may be more disinterested than the young because, as a consequence of their truncated horizon, they have less to gain from selfish behaviour.'[20] Alternatively, is it the nature of the learning curve that allows us to step off the treadmill only in old age? The nature of the learning curve may be such that decades of experience are required before we finally come to the conclusion that the treadmill is taking us nowhere. We are all familiar with the generosity of older people and their diminished acquisitiveness; and research shows that giving as a proportion of income increases with age.[21] Is this eventual stepping down off the treadmill evidence of a slow learning process? As the saying goes, there was never a person who, on their deathbed, declared that they regretted not having spent more time at work.

Whether or not these explanations of our unwillingness to step off the treadmill are correct, the important thing is that the consumption treadmill results in greater environmental degradation than would occur if it ceased to be a feature of contemporary society. The treadmill causes us to work more to enable us to consume more with the result that there is increased environmental disamenity; and it is this disamenity that distorts the work, leisure trade-off by giving us more than we bargained for when we make our earning and spending decisions.

THE TREADMILL AND INFORMATION ASYMMETRY

Earlier in this chapter it was foreshadowed that we would look at a caveat to the liberal position that, since consumers are the best judges of their own well-being, calls from critics of consumerism for individuals to alter their patterns of consumption are misplaced. This caveat is concerned with the issue of information limitations.

One of the market failures introduced in Chapter 2 was information limitations. The aspect of limited information that is most commonly dealt with by economists is information asymmetry – the situation where the most desirable market outcome does not occur because some parties to a transaction who have more, or better, information than others benefit from their information richness. One of the most researched aspects of this form of market failure in economics is the phenomenon of supplier-induced demand in the health industry.[22] The argument is that doctors and other health professionals who are information-rich can raise their incomes by overprescribing treatment for their information-poor patients.

In relation to the work, leisure trade-off, it can be argued that consumers are faced with a pervasive asymmetry of information that is manifested in a plethora of marketing and advertising which exhorts people to consume, and which sits alongside an almost complete absence of encouragement to people to put their feet up and relax. This asymmetry is, of course, exactly what we would expect in a capitalist society. Encouraging increased consumption produces enormous rewards for firms; encouraging leisure does not. There may be some benefits of increased leisure for firms that sell leisure-based consumption goods. However, as we've already noted, the major objective of these firms is to sell us something to use in our leisure time. They thus have an interest in us having as much purchasing power as possible (working as hard as possible) when not partaking of our leisure time activities.

Veblen, writing over 100 years ago, suggests another reason for the rise in consumption − as opposed to leisure − as a basis of impressing others. He argued that when communities were small and one's friends, acquaintances and fellow citizens were as likely to know as much about one's basking in leisure as they would about one's consumption then there was little to choose between each as a basis for impressing others. With the rise of communication and personal mobility, however, individuals are now in a position to impress a far larger group of persons. This widespread group will be in a far better position to observe the conspicuous consumption of the individual than to observe his or her partaking of leisure.[23]

If the behaviour of individuals is such that the asymmetry of information regarding the choice of consumption as opposed to leisure significantly tilts our preferences towards consumption, then this is a genuine case of market failure which warrants government intervention to correct it. In a way, it is not unlike the case of cigarette smoking where tobacco companies had a vested interest in encouraging us to smoke while no other significant private sector organization could profit from encouraging us to quit. As we know, in many countries the encouragement to quit was eventually funded by the state. In our discussion of policy proposals in Chapter 7 we will return to the issue of state intervention to correct the information asymmetry that promotes consumption but not leisure.

In the next chapter we return to the fundamental flaw so that an estimate can be made of the extent to which work hours should be reduced in order to negate its effects. The last word is given to Pope John Paul II.

The historical experience of the West, for its part, shows that even if the Marxist analysis and its foundation of alienation are false, nevertheless alienation − and the loss of the authentic meaning of life − is a reality in Western societies too. This happens in consumerism, when people are ensnared in a web of false and superficial gratifications rather than being helped to experience their personhood in an authentic and concrete way.[24]

NOTES

1   Veblen, T. (1899), *The Theory of the Leisure Class*, reprinted in part in Lerner, M. (1948), *The Portable Veblen*, New York: The Viking Press, p. 148.
2   Fukuyama, Francis (1992), *The End of History and the Last Man*, London: Penguin, p. 84.
3   Hirschman, A.O. (1982), *Shifting Involvements*, Princeton, New Jersey: Princeton University Press, p. 50.

4   Schor, J. (no date), 'The New Politics of Consumption', at http://www-polisci.mit.edu/
       BR24.3/schor/html, p. 5, accessed 13 July 2004.
5   A useful and insightful summary of these and other critiques of consumerism can be found
       in Heath, J. (1999), 'The structure of hip consumerism', at http://www.chass.utoronto.ca/
       philosophy/twp/9903/ twp_99_03_heath.html, accessed 6 December 2002. See also Shove,
       E. and Warde, A. (1998), 'Inconspicuous consumption: the sociology of consumption and
       the environment', Department of Sociology, Lancaster University, at http://www.comp.
       lancs.ac.uk/sociology/soc001aw.html, accessed 12 February 2002.
6   Cross, G. (1993), *Time and Money*, London: Routledge, p. 59.
7   Solow, Robert M. (1970), 'Science and Ideology in Economics', *The Public Interest*, Fall,
       reprinted in *Readings in Economics '73/'74* (1973), Guilford, CT: Annual Editions, p. 11.
8   See Heath (1999), pp. 6–8.
9   Although it can be argued that this assumption is made for similar reasons to those that
       form the basis for envy being considered a cardinal sin, this assumption is used primarily to
       enable the development of a tractable model of human behaviour. Recent contributions to
       the field of behavioural economics, in which much richer models of human behaviour are
       assumed, are slowly modifying this approach. See: Layard, Richard (2005), *Happiness*,
       New York: Penguin.
10   Hirsch, F. (1977), *The Social Limits to Growth*, London: Routledge & Keegan Paul.
11   Cross (1993), p. 196.
12   See, for example, Stiglitz, J.E. (2000), *Economics of the Public Sector*, 3rd ed., New York:
       W.W. Norton, Chap. 16.
13   McCracken quoted in Shove, E. and Warde, A. (1998), p. 9.
14   Heath (1999), pp. 8–10.
15   Lerner, M. (ed.) (1948), *The Portable Veblen*, New York: Viking Press, p. 81.
16   Buss quoted in Kasser, Tim (2002), *The High Price of Materialism*, Cambridge, MA: MIT
       Press, p. 2. Also see Frank, R.H. (1985), *Choosing the Right Pond: Human Behaviour and
       the Quest for Status*, New York: Oxford University Press, p. 19.
17   Easterlin, Richard A. (1974), 'Does Economic Growth Improve the human Lot? Some
       empirical Evidence', in David, P.A. and Reder, M.W. (eds), *Nations and Households in
       Economic Growth: Essays in Honor of Moses Abramovitz*, New York: Academic Press, pp.
       89–125, reproduced in Easterlin, Richard A. (2002), *Happiness in Economics*, Cheltenham,
       UK and Northampton, MA, USA: Edward Elgar, p. 29.
18   See Heath (1999), p. 7.
19   Kaufman, B.E. (1999), 'Expanding the Behavioural Foundations of Labor Economics',
       Industrial and Labor Relations Review, 52 (3), p. 379.
20   Posner, R.A. (1995), *Aging and old age*, Chicago: University of Chicago Press, p. 120.
21   See Independent Sector, *Giving and Volunteering in the United States*, at http://www.
       indepenedentsector.org/GandV/s_keyf.htm, accessed 15 May 2006.
22   See Phelps, Charles E. (2003), *Health Economics*, 3rd ed., Boston: Addison-Wesley, pp.
       236–247. More generally, services that are characterized by this asymmetry (including
       motor vehicle repairs and legal advice) are known in the literature as credence goods.
23   From *The Theory of the Leisure Class*, in Lerner, M. (ed.) (1948), p. 127.
24   From *Centesimus Annus*, para. 41 quoted in O'Boyle, E.J. (1997), 'A Commentary on John
       Paul II's Vision of the Social Economy', Annual Meetings of the Southwestern Economics
       Association, New Orleans, at http://www.cab.latech.edu/public/facstaff/Homes/oboyle/
       johnpaul/leisure.htm, accessed 14 July 2004.

5. Measuring the Cost of the Fundamental Flaw

The Gross National Product includes air pollution and advertising for cigarettes, and ambulances to clear our highways of carnage. It counts special locks for our doors, and jails for the people who break them. GNP includes the destruction of the redwoods and the death of Lake Superior. It grows with the production of napalm and missiles and nuclear warheads... And if GNP includes all this, there is much that it does not comprehend. It does not allow for the health of our families, the quality of their education, or the joy of their play. It is indifferent to the decency of our factories and the safety of our streets alike. It does not include the beauty of our poetry or the strength of our marriages, or the intelligence of our public debate or the integrity of our public officials... GNP measures neither our wit nor our courage, neither our wisdom nor our learning, neither our compassion nor our devotion to our country. It measures everything, in short, except that which makes life worthwhile.[1]

Robert Kennedy

In the previous chapters we have established that a fundamental flaw in the system, aided by the consumption treadmill, has resulted in an excess of work in relation to leisure that has reduced the well-being of the community. It has been argued that we would be happier if we had lower levels of income and consumption accompanied by a cleaner environment, less congestion and less stress.

But just how excessive is our work effort? One of the objectives of this chapter is to give an approximate idea of the extent to which work hours should be decreased if the effects of the fundamental flaw are to be eliminated. In estimating the reduction that is required we will be greatly assisted by the recent attempts by economists and others to develop indices of well-being and happiness. These indices are designed to replace, or at least supplement, traditional measures such as gross domestic product (GDP) which is the most widely used measure of national economic performance. We now look briefly at what GDP is, the role it plays in policy analysis, and criticisms of it as a measure of well-being.

WHAT IS GDP AND WHAT ARE ITS SHORTCOMINGS?

There is an enormous literature dealing with GDP and its shortcomings as a measure of well-being. As the introductory quote to this chapter from Senator Robert Kennedy shows, acknowledgement of these shortcomings has been in the public domain for a very long time

GDP, which is sometimes also described as national income, is a monetary measure of the total output of final goods and services in the economy. These final goods and services include consumption goods and services as well as investment goods like factories, mines and offices. These investment goods, along with labour and natural resources, make possible the current and future production of consumption goods and services. If we divide GDP by the nation's population we obtain a measure called GDP per capita.

Figures for GDP and GDP per capita have been of immeasurable value to policy-makers since they were first developed in the 1930s and 1940s. They can be used to measure the economic growth rate – the rate at which the nation and its population are developing economically over time – and they can be used to measure differences between nations in terms of their economic performance at any given time and over time. Conformity to a set of national income accounting standards assures that most countries calculate their GDP in the same way.

Unfortunately, GDP measures only one aspect of our well-being – the monetary value of the goods and services we produce. It is thus a poor indicator of quality of life (QOL). There are many different reasons given as to why GDP is a poor indicator of well-being. Although economists should be acutely aware of them – they are explained in detail in virtually every introductory economics text – the lack of a widely accepted alternative has meant that they continue to use GDP as the primary indicator of QOL.

Some of the shortcomings of GDP as a measure of well-being include the following:

1. The value of unpaid productive household activities – for example, cooking, cleaning and gardening – is not counted.
2. Increases in so-called defensive expenditures – for example, security measures to prevent crime, or reafforestation to make good destruction of natural forests – are counted although they are merely compensating for adverse human activities.
3. No account is taken of the costs of the reduction in leisure that permits increased work hours and a higher GDP.[2]
4. Pollution and the destruction of natural assets that are unmeasured costs of producing GDP are not subtracted.
5. Congestion that results in stress and increased unproductive time – especially on our roads – also involves costs that are not subtracted.

6. No account is taken of the wear and tear and obsolescence – otherwise known as depreciation – of the nation's man made capital stock.

The criticisms of GDP as a measure of well-being that will be emphasized here are those that look at cases where non-monetary costs that are incurred in producing GDP are not subtracted. The most important examples are the costs of pollution and degradation of environmental assets. Many of these costs are contributed to by urbanization and congestion. The English economist E.J. Mishan put the case for dispensing with GDP as a measure of welfare 40 years ago.

> Indices of economic growth may measure, in a rough sort of way, the increase in a country's gross productive power. But no provision is made in such indices for the 'negative goods' that are also being increased; that is, for the increasing burden of disamenities in the country…. Indeed, the adoption of economic growth as a primary aim of policy, whether it is urged upon us as a moral duty to the rest of the world or as a duty to posterity, or as a condition of survival, seems on reflection as likely to add, at least, as much 'ill-fare' as welfare to society.[3]

Furthermore, since Mishan wrote these words, a small band of economists interested in refining the assumptions about human behaviour that inform economic analysis have observed that individuals treat losses differently from gains – giving more weight to a given dollar amount of loss of wealth than is given to an equivalent dollar amount of gain. Foremost among these researchers are Khaneman and Tversky, the former, a psychologist who says he has never given an economics lecture in his life, being a recipient of the 2002 Nobel Prize for Economic Sciences.[4] The psychological propensity of individuals to weigh losses more highly than gains may help explain the grass roots revolt against many kinds of environmentally destructive activities that raise GDP, and it may help explain the 'paradox of progress' that sees GDP and human happiness moving in opposite directions over time.

Responding to the criticisms of GDP as a measure of well-being and to increasing evidence in support of Mishan's thesis that well-being may decline as GDP grows, a number of economists and others have developed alternative measures of national well-being.

ALTERNATIVE MEASURES OF WELL-BEING

Since the early 1970s a small but growing band of economists has set about developing indexes of well-being that can substitute for, or complement, GDP. Perhaps the best known index of well-being is the Genuine Progress Indicator (GPI) which has been calculated for the US. This index comes with impeccable credentials, being the successor to the Index of Sustainable

Economic Welfare (ISEW) developed by the doyen of ecological economists Herman Daly and his co-author John Cobb.

GPI is expressed in monetary terms so that its level at any time is directly comparable with GDP. In calculating GPI, the GDP of a nation can be taken as the starting point. Various additions to, and subtractions from, the GDP figure are then made. As we shall see, some of these subtractions involve explicit components of GDP that are deemed not to contribute to welfare. Being explicit components of GDP, they are expressed in monetary terms and reflect actual prices in the economy. The majority of additions and subtractions that must be made in order to calculate GPI are, however, implicit benefits and costs of human activity for which there are no actual prices in the economy that might be used as a basis for their calculation. In the case of these implicit benefits and costs, imputed values are estimated and expressed in monetary terms. Thus, for example, in calculating GPI an addition is made for the imputed monetary value of unpaid work in the household (child care, cleaning, gardening, etc.) and volunteer work. On the other hand, imputed values for pollution and congestion costs, and for depreciation of the man-made capital stock are subtracted when GPI is being calculated.

In calculating GPI, there are very few items that are actually added in. Most are cost items that are subtracted. These costs fall into two categories. First, there are the explicit costs that were described above as components of GDP that are deemed not to contribute to welfare. These include, for example, some defensive expenditures such as costs of automobile accidents and costs of household pollution abatement. The second category covers implicit costs that are incurred in producing GDP and which must be deducted to calculate GPI. These include the costs of water, noise and air pollution, depletion of non-renewable resources, loss of wetlands, farm land and old-growth forests, as well as the costs of long-term environmental damage and the costs of congestion. In addition to these costs, the calculation of GPI also involves subtraction of an implicit cost item that reflects the cost to the community of the depreciation of its stock of man-made capital. Subtractions are also made for an unequal distribution of income and for an item that reflects any increase in the US foreign debt.

Some measures of well-being, including the ISEW, also subtract part of annual expenditure on advertising. They do this on the basis that this advertising is designed primarily to create hitherto unexpressed desires for goods and services. Whether or not advertising does, indeed, do this is an issue we discussed, but did not resolve, in the previous chapter.

Other measures of well-being that have been developed include the Index of Well-being (IWB) and the Fordham Index of Social Health (FISH). There is a degree of variation between these measures resulting from differences of opinion as to the nature of the indicators that should be used to determine well-being. However, there is one feature that is common to almost all of them; namely, that they estimate that well-being in the US has not increased but has, in fact, declined over the past 30 years or more in spite of a very significant increase in per capita GDP.

WHAT THE ALTERNATIVE MEASURES SHOW

Figure 5.1 shows the movements of GPI and GDP for the period from 1950 to 2002. It is important to understand that because the figures for GPI and GDP are calculated in a different way, we would expect that GPI would always be less than GDP. What we would not expect, however, but what we actually find happening over the period, is the development of an ever-widening gap between the two measures. This ever-widening gap tells us that well-being has grown much more slowly over this period than has GDP. Put another way, GDP has increasingly become a misleading indicator of human welfare. (All figures in this graph are expressed in constant dollars, meaning that the figures are adjusted for inflation and are thus directly comparable no matter for which year they are quoted.)

Looking again at Figure 5.1 we see that in 1950, GDP per capita in the US was around $13 500 and GPI was estimated to be around $6 000. The difference of $5 500 is the value of the net subtractions from GDP that are required to convert it to GPI. By 2002, GDP per capita had more than tripled to be around $35 000 while GPI had only increased by around two-thirds to be approximately $10 000. In this year the net subtractions required to

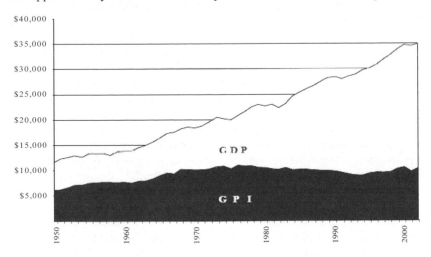

Source: Redefining Progress 2004

Figure 5.1 US GDP versus GPI, 1950–2002 ($ per capita)

convert GDP to GPI was a whopping $25 000. Remember that the difference between GDP and GPI is a net dollar measure of the amounts that need to be added to GDP to adjust for factors such as volunteer and household productive activities, and the amounts that need to be subtracted to adjust for factors like depreciation of the man-made capital stock, defensive expenditures, environmental degradation, congestion, and an unequal distribution of income. Over this 50-year period, a huge increase in sub-tractions has lead to an ever-widening gap between GDP and GPI. In large part, this ever-widening gap can be attributed to increasing implicit costs such as those associated with long-term environmental damage, depletion of non-renewable resources, pollution, congestion and urban sprawl.

A closer look at Figure 5.1 reveals that from 1950 until the mid-1970s, GPI closely tracked the movement of GDP, being roughly half of GDP throughout this period. From the mid-1970s, however, the measures start to diverge with continuing increases in GDP being associated with falling GPI for the greater part of the period to 2002. GDP per capita in the US has grown by approximately 75 per cent since the mid-1970s. Over that same period QOL as measured by the GPI per capita has essentially remained unchanged. The figures show that by 2002, approximately $15 000 more GDP per capita was being produced each year as compared to the mid-1970s; but this extra output, which was produced at great cost to both workers and the environment, brought no gain in QOL.

Evidence of the decline in QOL in the US over the second half of the 20th century is also supported by the finding, reported in *The American Paradox* by David Meyers, that the percentage of Americans who describe themselves as 'very happy' has not been exceeded since it peaked in 1957.[5] Further evidence of the decline comes from the authors of *Affluenza* who spoke to Marc Miringoff, custodian of the Fordham Index of Social Health (FISH). Miringoff told them that in the period from 1977 to 2000, the social health index had fallen by 45 per cent while GDP had risen by 79 per cent.[6]

A similar pattern of declining QOL, though sometimes less marked, has been observed in many other Western economies. Reporting on changes in the QOL in other countries, Richard Douthwaite tells us that the ISEW has fallen in both Germany and the UK over the past 20 years or more. He also reports that, notwithstanding Ireland's rapid GDP growth in recent times, a FISH index for Ireland has also fallen over this period.[7]

Paradoxically, the falls in QOL that have occurred in these countries can be explained by the rises in GDP per capita that have brought with them increased congestion, urban sprawl, increased pollution and general environmental degradation. The greater the sacrifices that are made to produce more output per capita, the greater is the extent to which we compromise work-life balance and the lower is our well-being. But why have we bothered to work at much the same pace as previously, or even harder as Schor argues is the case in the US, when this has resulted in increases in GDP per capita that cause no increase in QOL?[8] We could have worked less, had less money income and less consumption while at the same time reaping the benefits of less environmental degradation, less congestion and less stress that detract from QOL. In short, we could have had more leisure *and* a higher QOL. As we have seen, this unfortunate outcome has occurred as a result of a fundamental flaw in market economies.

In the next section we look to measure the extent to which we are currently reducing our well-being by engaging in too much work and too little leisure.

COUNTING THE COST OF TOO MUCH WORK AND TOO LITTLE LEISURE

In the previous chapters we have demonstrated that because of a fundamental flaw in the economy we are duped into working too much. The reason that we do this is that we compare the unpleasantness of work with the monetary benefits it brings without taking into account the negative externalities that accompany production and consumption. These negative externalities, which include environmental disamenity, urban sprawl and congestion, can be measured by calculating their *implicit costs*; that is, the costs they indiscriminately impose on society. These implicit costs, from which each of us suffers to a greater or lesser degree, are the selfsame costs that economists who calculate indexes of well-being like the GPI subtract from GDP to arrive at a monetary value of well-being.

There may also be significant *explicit costs* that are not generated by negative externalities but which we, nonetheless, fail to debit against money income from our work effort because we fail to see the connection between the two. Examples include the increased cost of medical care if our increased work effort increases stress levels, or increased purchases of take-out meals if increased work effort means we have less time and energy to prepare meals in the home. It would be argued by ultra liberals that it would not be consistent with the liberal economic position to assert that explicit costs such as these are not taken into account by individuals when determining the amount of work effort to undertake. On the other hand, it could be argued that failure to take these costs into account represents a case of bounded rationality which was described, in Chapter 4, as the inability to compute what is objectively in our best interest in a highly complex world. Either way, in the overall scheme of things these explicit costs are judged by those who construct alternative economic indicators of well-being to be of far less magnitude than the implicit costs of environmental degradation and congestion. Accordingly, in the analysis that follows, we make the cautious assumption that workers are fully aware of all the explicit costs generated by their work effort.

Our task is thus to concentrate on determining the dollar value of the implicit costs of environmental degradation and congestion that are the result of the production and consumption activities that occur in the economy. We are doing this so that we can compare the money income of workers – which they use as the basis for determining the extent of their work effort – with these 'hidden' costs.

In determining the implicit costs of environmental degradation and of congestion we are ignoring many other implicit costs that are deducted in the process of calculating GPI. These include the costs of an unequal distribution of income, costs of national foreign indebtedness, and the costs of family breakdown. We do this because we are concentrating, as was explained in Chapter 1, on the link between work effort and environmental and congestion costs.

Fortunately, the data used to calculate GPI contains good estimates of the implicit costs we are looking for. There are estimates of total annual environmental costs for the US which include costs for water, air and noise pollution, loss of wetlands, farms and forests, depletion of non-renewable resources and ozone, and long-term environmental damage. These annual costs amounted to approximately $3920 billion in 2002. There is also an estimate of the annual costs of congestion in the form of commuting costs. However, given that some of these commuting costs will be explicit costs that are not externalities but direct costs incurred willingly by commuters, it would be safer to exclude this estimate from our analysis. For the record, these costs amounted to $484 billion in 2002.

The total annual environmental cost of $3920 billion in 2002 is equivalent to about $13 000 per capita. This is more than a third of the GDP per capita of $35 000 generated in that year. These data are telling us that because there are very large implicit environmental costs of producing and consuming GDP, well-being is significantly less than the figure for GDP would suggest. In order to determine the extent to which workers undertake excessive work effort because they look at money incomes alone without deducting implicit environmental costs, we must now compare these costs with workers' earnings. But to what extent can these costs be attributed to the production and consumption that are enabled by the work effort of individuals?

Approximately 75 per cent of GDP in the US is contributed to by labour.[9] To determine the extent to which this labour activity contributes to the total implicit environmental and congestion costs experienced in the US would be a daunting task. Nonetheless, an approximation is required here. For want of a better estimate, it is assumed that the contribution of labour to the annual environmental cost of $3920 billion is proportional to its contribution to GDP. Thus labour's contribution is calculated to be $2940 billion (0.75 × $3920). To the extent that machines and factories contribute more production-based environmental costs to the economy than do workers, this will be an overestimate. On the other hand, to the extent that consumption-based environmental and congestion costs are generated by workers rather than machines it will be an underestimate.

When workers make a decision as to the degree of work effort to undertake (the hours they work) they compare work effort not with their pre-tax money income but with their lower post-tax or personal disposable money income. In 2002 personal disposable money income in the US was approximately $7080 billion. This disposable money income includes a small proportion of non-labour income earned by individuals – the income that comes from investment by individuals in stocks and bonds, rental properties, small businesses and so on. While most of this income does not derive from current work effort, it is easy to see that in sacrificing consumption so as to save for these investments, individuals are being short-changed in the same way that they are short-changed when they earn labour income. When individuals receive a monetary return from their investments, they also get environmental disamenity that is produced by the mines, machines and factories that these investments represent. As we shall see later in this chapter, to determine the true value of these investments to individuals we would need to subtract the costs of this environmental disamenity from the gross monetary income earned from them.

With a total implicit environmental cost of $2940 billion attributed to labour in 2002 set against personal disposable income of approximately $7080 billion in that year, it can be seen that the environmental cost constitutes 40 per cent of the value of personal disposable income.[10]

Expressing this in a different way, every after-tax dollar of income earned and spent by a typical American is associated with 40 cents of environmental cost. Workers receiving an after-tax money wage of $20 per hour receive the equivalent of $12 when we take into account the implicit environmental costs. Someone earning $100 per hour after tax is really only receiving $60 per hour as compensation for their work effort. This lower compensation for work effort which takes into account the implicit environmental costs will be described here as the environmentally adjusted income (EAI).

Because we think we are earning almost twice the actual benefit to us of our work effort – because the EAI is little more than half of our money wage – there is a significant bias towards work as opposed to leisure.

This bias is found in every nation but will, of course, be more pronounced in countries where environmental disamenity is high in relation to the level of wages. Within each country, there may also be significant differences in this adjusted income between different locations. Thus, for a given wage level, the adjusted income is likely to be lower in crowded and polluted cities than in rural areas. But if cities are characterized by greater environmental disamenity and a lower adjusted income, why do we observe the tendency in some countries for population to continue to migrate to the city? The obvious answer is that the range of goods, services, jobs and lifestyle experiences available in the city is greater. A less obvious answer is that migrants are attracted because wages are typically higher in the city. If, however, greater environmental disamenity in the city means that city dwellers' adjusted incomes are *lower* although their wages are *higher* the upshot is that migrants from rural areas are being misled if they ignore differences in environmental disamenity and react only to differences in wages. In developing countries, one often hears disparaging remarks about poor migrants who have moved from the countryside to the cities only to discover that their QOL is lower and the streets are not paved with gold. Unfortunately, this is all too often a one-way street as the communities from which the out-migration occurs are destroyed in the process.

In their pioneering work on an alternative to GDP as a measure of welfare, Nordhaus and Tobin observed that '[s]ome portion of the higher earnings of urban residents may be simply compensation for the disamenities of urban life and work.'[11] They go on to argue that if this is so we should not count as a gain of welfare the full increments of GDP that result from an individual moving from farm or small town to city. Support for Nordhaus and Tobin's position may also be inferred from the oft expressed desire of retirees to move away from cities that previously provided their employment.

All of this is not to say that there are not some individuals who do take into account the effects of environmental disamenity on the value of the incomes they and their fellow human beings earn. There is a small number of committed environmentalists who do consciously take the environmental costs of their activities into account and choose to live an alternative lifestyle involving a limited work effort. Nonetheless, the problem of overwork is unwittingly contributed to by virtually all members of the work force.

BY HOW MUCH SHOULD OUR WORK HOURS FALL?

If we are really working for an environmentally adjusted income (EAI) that is 60 per cent of our money income, by how much should our work hours be reduced? Fortunately, there is a large body of economic research that can guide us in our endeavours. However, we should exercise caution in using this research because it typically examines the effects of much smaller changes in remuneration than the 40 per cent we are dealing with here.

There are two steps that need to be undertaken to determine the decrease in the number of hours worked that would result from a realization that, as a result of the fundamental flaw, we are really being remunerated far less than our money wages suggest. They are:

1. Determine the extent to which workers reduce their willingness to work because of the combination of the substitution and income effects that were explained in Chapter 2. This is a measure of the decrease in the

supply of labour that results from realization that the EAI is far lower than money wages.

2. Determine the extent to which this decrease in the supply of labour raises money wages in the labour market because labour is now scarcer. A rise in money wages will mean that the initial decrease in willingness to work as a result of the combined income and substitution effects outlined above will be moderated to some extent.

Step 1

Recall that in Chapter 2 we explained that a fall in wages brings two opposing forces into play. The first of these is the substitution effect that tends to reduce willingness to work because leisure is substituted for the lower paid work. The second is the income effect which tends to increase willingness to work because the lower rate of pay means that the luxury of leisure is less affordable. When there are no 'hidden' externality-based costs associated with production and consumption of goods and services, a decrease in money wages results in these effects working in opposite directions. They tend to cancel each other out to a greater or lesser degree.

However, when we take account of the externality-based costs that accompany production and consumption, there is a turbo-charged effect brought about by the income and substitution effects reinforcing each other. Not only does the replacement of the money wage with the lower EAI as a basis for decision-making decrease willingness to work through the substitution effect but the subsequent rise in QOL also discourages willingness to work through the income effect. (Because we *feel* better off we demand more of the luxury of leisure time.)

Looking first at economists' studies that take account of both the substitution effect and the income effect when these effects are based on changes in money incomes alone and are thus working in opposite directions, we find that in developed countries a 10 per cent fall in income results in a decrease in willingness to work of between 1 per cent and 3 per cent.[12] If we use figure of 2 per cent, which is the midpoint of this range, a 40 per cent decrease in income to its EAI level would bring about an 8 per cent decrease in willingness to work.

However, because this estimate does not take into account the increase in QOL that would result from a significant reduction in output, consumption and environmental degradation that would accompany such a reduction in willingness to work, it understates the degree to which work effort would decrease. Although economists do not have estimates of the responsiveness of labour to such compensating QOL effects, they do have estimates of the responsiveness of labour to decreases in wages that are compensated by lump-sum increases in money income that are not related to willingness to work (for example, from government welfare benefits). The midpoint of these estimates suggest that a 10 per cent fall in income would result in a 3.5 per cent fall in willingness to work.[13] If we were to assume that the increase in QOL consequent upon a fall in willingness to work exactly compensated for the fall in money income that this lower willingness to work occasioned, then this figure of 3.5 per cent would be more relevant. (Our basic argument, as Figure 3.1 in Chapter 3 indicated, is that it would more than compensate; in which case the responsiveness would be even greater.) If we use the conservative figure of 3.5 per cent, a 40 per cent fall in income would give rise to a 14 per cent decrease in willingness to work (3.5 × 0.4).

As was briefly explained in Chapter 2, because this turbo-charged effect also works in the opposite direction, it may be a factor that helps to explain the phenomenon of the 'overworked American'. As money incomes have risen over the last few decades, the substitution effect has encouraged greater willingness to work; furthermore, at the same time, the decline in QOL as indicated by the GPI and other measures of well-being has made wage earners work longer hours because they feel worse off and less able to afford the luxury of leisure. The idea that a decrease in QOL would increase our willingness to work is consistent with psychologist Tim Kasser's findings that low QOL associated with divorce or low socio-economic family status is positively correlated with materialism. Children of families with a low QOL have more materialistic values than those from families with a high QOL.[14]

We can explain the tendency for a falling QOL to encourage increased work effort in an alternative way by extending Marshall's treatment of the berry-picking boy that was introduced in Chapter 2.

Imagine that a permanent change in the microclimate means that henceforth the tastiness of berries increases significantly. Because the resulting pleasure from each act of picking a berry has increased, this is, in effect, an increase in the boy's wage. Marshall's boy will thus put in more work effort to pick more berries (the substitution effect). Now let us suppose that, unfortunately, this extra effort by the boy results in disturbance to the habitat of beautiful songbirds whose numbers are, as a result, severely depleted. The boy notices the absence of the birds and their beautiful voices but he does not understand the connection between his increased work effort and this loss. If the loss of pleasure from the birds' song is greater than the extra pleasure he has derived from the extra work effort he has undertaken (the extra berries he has picked) during this berry season, his well-being or QOL is lower than in previous years. In the language we used earlier in this chapter, his GDP has gone up but his GPI has gone down. Because he feels less well off, when the next berry season comes around he feels that he cannot afford the luxury of leisure to the degree that he has enjoyed it in the past. As a result, he puts in more work effort (the income effect). The higher wages in the form of sweeter berries have increased his work effort; but so too has the net decline in well-being or QOL that was brought about by the excess of the cost of the loss of songbirds over the additional net benefit of more sweeter berries. The boy's QOL would have been higher if he could have been educated to see the error of his ways or if a limit to his work effort had been mandated.

Unfortunately, if the reduction in his QOL that resulted from fewer song birds had been partly or wholly the result of a negative externality created by another berry-picking boy in the same neighbourhood, this education programme would only be partially successful if it applied to the first boy alone. Recall that in Chapter 3 we pointed out that there is no incentive for individuals who recognize the fundamental flaw and its effects to unilaterally reduce their work effort – their decision to go it alone would have no significant effect on the overall level of environmental disamenity caused by excessive work effort on the part of the total workforce. Thus, even if both of our berry-picking boys are educated in the error of their ways, it is still the case that if either or both of them considered that a go-it-alone reduction in their work effort would not prevent the songbird population from being severely depleted anyway, they would not make the reduction in work effort. Remember, they are both on a 'forced ride' to somewhere (a neighbourhood devoid of bird song) that they don't want to go.

Step 2

Recall that in this step our objective is to determine the extent to which the reduction in willingness to work calculated in Step 1 would be moderated by the increase in money wages that would occur as a consequence of the reduced supply of labour in the labour market. We have already estimated in Step 1 that a 40 per cent fall in income would give rise to a 14 per cent decrease in willingness to work. As has already been explained, the complexities of the labour market mean that a 14 per cent decrease in willingness to work does not necessarily translate into an equivalent percentage decrease in hours worked. This is because an intended decrease in willingness to work on the part of workers would result in employers paying higher money wages that would to some extent discourage workers from reducing hours worked. (The increased scarcity of labour would raise its price.) Economists' estimates of the extent to which employers would respond to an intended decrease in willingness to work by raising wages vary greatly within and between different countries. However, the estimates used in models of national economies suggest that the reduction in hours worked is likely to be about half of the decrease in willingness to work. That is, a 14 per cent decrease in willingness to work is likely to decrease hours worked by about 7 per cent.

Our conclusion is thus that if, in making decisions about their work effort, workers were to take into account their EAI rather than their current money income there would be a national reduction of work hours of approximately 7 per cent. If an education programme could teach all workers to reduce their willingness to work to such an extent that this 7 per cent decrease in hours worked was achieved, this would mean that the effect of the fundamental flaw would be eliminated. However, for reasons that will be discussed in Chapter 7, where policy alternatives are examined, there are a number of impediments to the introduction of such an education programme. In Chapter 7, mandated shorter working hours will be recommended as the primary policy approach that flows from the arguments in this book.

If a mandated decrease in work hours is the chosen policy, this can be brought about in a variety of ways. If all who currently work were to continue to do so, their work hours on average would need to decrease by roughly 2.8 hours per 40 hours worked. A 40-hour week could become a 37.2 hour week, or a 50-week working year could be reduced to 46.5 weeks. Alternatively, the same outcome could be achieved by a smaller reduction in the number of hours worked accompanied by a lower rate of participation in the work force. This may come about as a result of developments such as earlier retirement, extended parenting leave, or decreased participation of men in the work force. A reduction of work effort of the magnitude suggested here would, as we shall argue in the policy chapter, need to be staged if serious short-term dislocation of the economy were to be avoided.

Up to this point we have been analysing the extent to which we engage in excessive hours of formal work. But labour is only one of a number of sources of GDP, albeit the largest. Recall that it contributes about three quarters of the GDP of developed nations. The other major contributors to GDP are natural resources and capital. Since a major objective of this book is to advance arguments that will help eliminate excessive use of natural resources, it is appropriate that we think of them as the primary input to GDP which is transformed by productive processes involving inputs of labour and capital. The theme that we have pursued so far here is that smaller inputs of labour (fewer hours of work) will reduce the call upon these primary natural resource inputs. But, you might say, what about the inputs of capital? Won't they continue to wreak havoc on the environment and on our QOL at an undiminished rate? In the next section we see how reducing the hours that individuals work brings with it a decreased role for capital in despoiling the environment.

WHAT ABOUT CAPITAL?

Capital is the mostly long-lived, man-made contributor to the productive processes. It is typified by buildings, factories, machines, vehicles and communication networks. There is good capital and bad. There is enormous scope for policy innovations to gradually bring about change in the nature of capital employed in environmentally sensitive activities. These changes, many of which are the outcome of technological advancement, have the

potential to greatly reduce the degree of environmental degradation per unit
of output. This is a process that has been under way for centuries but which
has accelerated in the recent past. A prominent example of these changes is
the reduction in pollution from motor vehicles as a result of increased fuel
economy, the use of unleaded gasoline, and the use of catalytic converters
that reduce exhaust emissions. As will be argued in Chapter 7, measures such
as these are an important part of the ongoing ad hoc policy thrust that must
accompany reduced work hours if sustainability is to be achieved. On their
own, however, these measures will not be enough. Although they have the
potential to reduce environmental degradation in some areas, they can have
little impact in others. How much potential is there, for example, for warfare
to become less environmentally degrading? The long course of history has
shown it to have ever increasing adverse environmental effects.

Furthermore, it is likely that some newly developed capital equipment that
is designed to be environmentally friendly will be found, in the long run, to
be just the opposite. Already, wind farms − those banks of high-tech
windmills that seem to be forever springing up in the world's windiest places
− are displaying an unforseen malevolence. Increasingly, they are considered
to be despoiling pristine coastal environments, interfering with sites of
historical importance, or desecrating land of spiritual significance to
indigenous communities.

Ad hoc policies that reduce the adverse environmental effects of capital
have only limited efficacy. Fortunately, however, a decrease in work hours
can be expected to bring about a decrease in the total amount of capital in the
economy with beneficial environmental effects. Fewer work hours means less
GDP, less saving and less investment in capital.[15]

SO MUCH STUFF, SO LITTLE TIME

'Speed dating' is the latest commercial way to find a partner. Apparently, an
activity that previously took days, weeks or months can now be undertaken in
10 minutes or less. Dating agencies bring a group of people together at a
suitable venue where each person has up to 10 minutes to speak to each of
the other members of the group to see if they can find a compatible partner.[16]

This is just one manifestation of a time-poor society. The others are
familiar enough. Comments like 'we didn't get to use all of those prepaid
tickets to the theatre' or 'the new set of golf clubs hasn't had much exercise'
or 'that new cook book I purchased has only been opened once' are
commonplace. As *Barron's* Assistant Managing Editor, Lauren Rublin
explains, we have too many consumer goods and too little time to use them:

As Americans collectively grow older, more prosperous and more stressed, increasing numbers are reaching the same conclusion: As a nation, we have a surfeit of 'stuff', but an alarming dearth of time for ourselves and each other.[17]

Corroborating evidence comes from Juliet Schor who quotes Robinson and Godby's finding that the proportion of the population that 'always feels rushed' has grown from 24 per cent in 1965 to 32 per cent in 1997 with a peak of 38 per cent in 1992.[18] In a review of Carl Honoré's *In Praise of Slow*, Piers Moore Ede points out Honoré's findings that 'Americans now spend forty per cent less time with their children than they did in the 1960s. The average man spends seventy-two minutes of every day behind the wheel of a car. A typical business executive now loses sixty-eight hours a year to being put on hold, and American adults currently devote on average a meagre half-hour per week to making love.' He also points out that 'fatigue has contributed to some of the world's worst disasters, including Chernobyl, Exxon-Valdez, and Three Mile Island.'[19]

The comprehensive economic theory of the allocation of time which was pioneered by Nobel Prize winning economist Gary Becker, tells us that, for each consumer, there will be an optimum ratio of consumer goods to availability of leisure time in which to use them.[20] For example, too few goods and too much time on our hands would lead to corrective action involving more work, less leisure and more goods to use in our reduced leisure time. In this book we are dealing with the opposite case where the fundamental flaw has led to too many goods but too little leisure time in which to use them. We have been duped into working excessively long hours with the result that we produce too many consumer goods that we can't find time to use and that clutter up our houses. This clutter has spawned a whole industry devoted to alleviating its effects. In 2005 there were at least three reality shows on US cable TV dealing with clutter management; perhaps the best known of these is the Learning Channel's 'Clean Sweep'. Unfortunately, the oft suggested solution of being self-disciplined enough to throw away offending items is the worst possible solution. The environmentally correct solution, of course, is not to purchase the offending items in the first place. Apart from increased environmental amenity, less work and less consumption means less clutter at home.

Another way to look at the problem of too much stuff and too little time is to think of the value of our leisure time as being measured by the income (wage) we give up in order to have it. If we were to place a lower value on our leisure time than is indicated by our money wage because we realize that the EAI is significantly lower than the money wage, we could be expected to engage in more time-intensive and fewer goods-intensive leisure activities. This is because we now realize that the time costs us significantly less while the cost of the goods remains largely unchanged.

Less work and more leisure would alleviate the problem of too much stuff and too little time. However, the full benefits of such a change would not occur immediately because we have been amassing consumer goods at an excessive rate for a very long time. Nonetheless, imagine that, all of a sudden, you had an additional two or three hours a week to use the consumer goods you already own – to play a round of golf or to try that recipe from the book. In terms of more efficient use of consumer goods, the benefits of more leisure time would be immediate. But these benefits would grow as the ratio of our stock of consumer goods to our leisure time decreased over time; and they would persist indefinitely, as would the less immediate benefits of increased environmental amenity and less congestion.

Finally, it is important to understand that the reduced work effort that occurs when we wise-up to the full environmental costs of present levels of production does not mean that the reduced work effort eliminates environmental degradation and its costs. Recall from Chapter 3 that basing our work effort on the EAI reduces work effort and increases the difference between happiness from work and unhappiness from work. At the same time, it decreases the total costs imposed on the environment but does not eliminate them. In the light of the importance of the assimilative capacity of the environment discussed in Chapter 2, this reduction may well bring many aspects of environmental degradation within this capacity. Furthermore, as we shall see in the next chapter, this present reduction in degradation of the environment may pay very large dividends for future generations. This chapter commenced with a quote from Robert Kennedy outlining the shortcomings of GDP as a measure of well-being; the last word is given to John F. Kennedy:

> I look forward to an America which will not be afraid of grace and beauty, which will protect the beauty of our national environment, which will preserve the great old American houses and squares and parks of our national past and which will build handsome and balanced cities for our future. [21]

NOTES

1   Kennedy, Robert F. (1968) from a speech; quoted in Anielski, M. (2000), 'Fertile Obfuscation: Making Money Whilst Eroding Living Capital', paper presented at the 34th Annual Conference of the Canadian Economics Association, University of British Columbia, Vancouver, BC, 2–4 June at http://members.shaw.ca/GD2004/2004 Work Anielski.htm, p.6 accessed 30 January 2006.
2   Similarly, no account is taken of the benefits of *increases* in leisure time which result in a *lower* level of GDP.
3   Mishan, E.J. (1969), *The Costs of Economic Growth*, Harmondsworth: Pelican, p. 64.
4   See Tauberer, Joshua (2002), 'Kahneman wins Nobel Prize in economics for behavioural study', The Daily Princetonian, 10 October at http://www.dailyprincetonian. com/archives /2002/10/10/news /5684.shtml, accessed 15 July 2004.
5   Myers, D.G. (2000), *The American Paradox*, New Haven: Yale University Press, p. 136. Also see Layard, Richard (2005), *Happinesss*, New York: Penguin, pp. 29–30.

6   de Graff, J., Wann, D. and Naylor, T. D. (2001), *Affluenza*, San Francisco: Berrett-Khoeler, p. 66.
7   Douthwaite, R. (1998), 'Good Growth and Bad Growth', at http://www.csf.colorado.edu/ecol-econ/good_ bad_growth.douthwaite.html, accessed 18 February 2003. By contrast, Richard Layard tells us that in many continental European countries there has been a slight upward trend in happiness since 1975 but that '[o]verall, the change in happiness is small relative to the huge increase in incomes.' Layard, p. 30.
8   Schor, Juliet (1992), *The Overworked American*, New York: Basic Books.
9   Dornbusch, R., Fischer, S. and Startz, R. (2001), *Macroeconomics, International Edition*, Singapore, McGraw-Hill, p. 47.
10   All figures quoted in this section are expressed in constant 1996 dollars.
11   Daly, H.E., and Cobb, J.B. (1989), *For the Common Good*, Boston: Beacon Press, p. 78.
12   These figures come from a study by Resources for the Future economist Ian Parry. See Parry, I.W.H. (2001), 'On the Costs of Excise Taxes and Income Taxes in the UK', at http ://www.rff.org/~parry/Papers/MEB_UK.pdf, accessed 16 July 2004.
13   Ibid.
14   Kasser, Tim (2002), *The High Price of Materialism*, Cambridge, MA: MIT Press, p. 32.
15   A little reflection reveals that in the same way that monetary returns from work effort should be discounted because of the adverse external effects of production and consumption, so the returns to capital should be similarly discounted. The fact that some mutual funds are able to successfully offer portfolios of stocks selected on the basis of ethical or green criteria suggests that some investors acknowledge and act upon the production externalities at least.
16   A search for 'speed dating' in a web browser gave 3, 670 000 hits at the end of 2005.
17   Rublin, L. (1998), 'Too much, Too Much!', *Barron's*, March 9.
18   Schor, Juliet (1997), 'Civic engagement and working hours: do Americans really have more free time than ever before?', Conference on Civic Engagement in American Democracy, Portland Maine, 26–28 September at http://www.swt.org/putok.htm, accessed 16 July 2004.
19   Ede, Piers Moore (no date), 'A Paean to Pleasure', Resurgence at http://www.resurgence.org /bookshelf/ede1005.htm, accessed 30 November 2005.
20   Becker, Gary S. (1965), 'A Theory of the Allocation of Time', *The Economic Journal*, **75** (299), 493–517.
21   Kennedy, John F. (1963), Speech at Amherst College, Massachusetts to praise American poet Robert Frost, 27 October at http://www.cc.gatech.edu/people/home/idris/Speeches/kennedy_frost.htm, accessed 16 July 2004.

6. The Cumulative Effect and International Differences

[T]here commenced in the eighteenth century and reached a climax in the nineteenth century a new view of the functions of the State and society, which still governs us today. This view was the utilitarian and economic – one might almost say financial – ideal, as the sole, respectable purpose of the community as a whole; the most dreadful heresy, perhaps, which has ever gained the ear of a civilized people. Bread and nothing but bread, and not even bread, and bread accumulating at compound interest until it has turned to stone.[1]

J.M. Keynes

The quotation above comes from the most celebrated economist of the 20th century. He continues with these words.

[T]he Treasury view has prevailed. Not only in practice. The theory is equally powerful. We have persuaded ourselves that it is positively wicked for the State to spend a halfpenny on non-economic purposes.... If there arise some occasion of non-economic expenditure which it would be a manifest public scandal to forego, it is thought suitable to hand round the hat to solicit the charity of private persons. This expedient is sometimes applied in cases which would be incredible if we were not so well accustomed to them. An outstanding example is to be found where the preservation of the countryside from exploitation is required for reasons of health, recreation, amenity, or natural beauty.[2]

The environmental and congestion problems that confront us today have been with us for centuries. Their significance has been exacerbated by the rise of the utilitarian and economic ideal that Keynes so detested, by population growth and by technological, political and cultural changes that have enabled and promoted enormous growth in economic activity. Another major reason for this increasing burden of environmental degradation and congestion is that the fundamental flaw has also been with us for centuries. Its importance increased enormously in the 18th and 19th centuries with the movement of work from cottage, village and farm to urban environs where the capacity of urban workers to detect and act upon the negative externalities associated with their work processes was greatly diminished. In the 18th century Oliver Goldsmith dealt with these issues in his poem *The Deserted Village*:

A time there was, ere England's griefs began,
When every rood of ground maintained its man;
For him light labour spread her wholesome store,
Just gave what life required, but gave no more:
His best companions, innocence and health;
And his best riches, ignorance of wealth.

The fundamental flaw which arose during the industrial revolution has been further exacerbated in the past half a century: the easily detected and easily remedied negative externalities associated with home-based productive activities have increasingly been replaced by those associated with market activities as a greater proportion of adults have joined the work force.

Alfred Marshall chose carefully his blackberry-picking example that we used in Chapter 2 to explain the relationship between the displeasure of work and the pleasure of the consumption it enables. The berry-picker in this example was able to compare directly the costs of his work effort with its pleasurable results. Likewise the workers of yore in cottage industries, or undertaking home-based productive activities were well placed to compare the individual benefits of their work effort with its costs − including the negative externalities that might flow from it.[3] With the rise of the factory system in the west and the concomitant displacement of work from home and village to cities and towns, the relationship between work and the negative externalities it caused was, however, severed. Workers looked only at the relationship between the monetary reward in the form of wages that they received, and the individual work effort they undertook. Although they observed environmental disamenity all around them, its connection with their individual work effort was either lost or perceived to be beyond their control. The fundamental flaw had come into play. Witness these descriptions of life in the US in the last quarter of the 19th century.

> The urban streets of the 1870s and 1880s were full not just of horses but pigs, which were tolerated because they ate garbage....The increasing production of animal waste caused pessimistic observers to fear that American cities would disappear like Pompeii − but not under ashes. Added to that was acrid industrial smog, sidewalks piled high with kitchen slops, coal dust, and dumped merchandise.... Rudyard Kipling said of Chicago, 'Having seen it I desire urgently never to see it again. Its air is dirt'.

> Coal miners, steel workers, and many others worked 60-hour weeks in dirty and dangerous conditions, exposed to suffocating gas and smoke. Danger was not confined to mines or mills; in 1890 one railroad employee was killed for every 300 employed.[4]

The environmental degradation of the day was not, of course, confined to the cities. More permanent effects were being wrought in the countryside where old growth forests in the Americas, in Australasia and in parts of Asia were mercilessly exploited to provide timber for construction and for fuel. Robert Gordon quotes David and Wright who point out that half of the non-residential investment in the US in 1850 was constituted by clearing of forests and preparation of previously forested land for agriculture.[5]

Modern day manifestations of these problems can be observed in many rapidly industrializing countries where increased manufacturing, the movement of population to the cities, and logging are having profound environmental effects.

The purpose of this chapter is to investigate the cumulative effects of this disjunction of work effort from the environmental and congestion problems it causes. The fundamental flaw has been with us since at least the commencement of the industrial revolution. This means that we have been engaging in work effort in excess of that which would maximize our QOL for more than two centuries.

COMPOUNDING THE PROBLEM OR BREAD INTO STONE

Many critics of consumerism describe the multitude of apparently unnecessary material goods that we buy as stuff. Stuff is the modern term for the bread that Keynes described as accumulating at compound interest until it turns into stone. For a national economy, the accumulation of production over time is measured by compounding the annual growth rate of the economy; and here we are thinking about the growth of GDP which, notwithstanding the fact that it is a very poor measure of QOL, is the best measure we have of the environment-sapping production of goods and services in the economy.

Consistent with our analysis up to this point, in which we have been looking at work effort on the part of the individual worker rather than aggregate work effort in the economy, we need to compound annual rates of growth of GDP *per capita* in order to see how much more stuff per person we might produce today as compared to a decade or a century or two centuries ago. If we compare actual growth in per capita GDP over the past, say, 100 years with the growth that would have prevailed if we had recognized and acted upon the fundamental flaw 100 years ago, we can determine by how much current production exceeds the level that would otherwise have prevailed.

In the analysis that follows a cautious approach is being undertaken. The assumptions that we use will bias the outcomes in such a way as to ensure that we do not overestimate the excess of current production over the level that would have prevailed if the fundamental flaw had been recognized.

Counting the Cumulative Cost of Too Much Work and Too Little Leisure

Explaining the emergence of a democratic basis for the determination of the division between work and leisure, Gary Cross points out that by the late 1880s, there had emerged throughout the industrial world a loose coalition, made up of social liberals and trade unionists, that forcefully advocated the democratic share-out of time and money.[6] Prior to this time, the choice of consumption versus leisure was in the hands of elites such as factory and mill owners, the crown, and governments with limited franchise.[7] Because these elites could protect themselves from the worst aspects of environmental pollution and degradation, and because they wielded great power in relation to workers, it is probable that the extent to which work was excessive in relation to leisure was greater at that time than it is today. This is supported by the observation that developing countries that are experiencing rapid industrialization today have a much higher level of pollution per dollar of GDP than do the developed nations.[8] In order to avoid these complications and because, as Cross points out, the labour movement has, generally speaking, only been in a position to determine labour's hours of work since the end of the 19th century, in the analysis that follows we shall give emphasis to the extent to which excessive work effort has compounded GDP per capita over the past century. Further, we shall assume that this excessive work effort was the same in every year. (In reality, it would have been higher during the war years and much lower during the Great Depression.) There are some heroic assumptions in this analysis. However, confirmation of the idea that we suffer from a compounding of the problem is what we are trying to get across here rather than some precise estimate of the extent of that compounding.

In the previous chapter we estimated that maximization of QOL consequent upon recognition of the fundamental flaw would require a reduction in work effort to a level that is approximately 7 per cent below the current level. Just what a 7 per cent reduction in work effort by all individuals would mean in terms of reduced output is a moot point. There is no reason to go into the factors that might explain why the end result of such a reduction would be a fall in GDP per capita that was more or less than the 7 per cent fall in work effort. All that we need to be sure about is that reduced work effort by all individuals in the economy means reduced GDP per capita. For the sake of illustration, we will simply assume that the fall in GDP per capita is proportional to the fall in work hours. Readers may do their own calculations based on different assumptions about this relationship. The reader is also cautioned that because reliable measures of GDP and GDP per capita have been available for developed countries only since World War II, the estimates of annual growth in GDP per capita that we are using here are approximate.

In terms of its effect on annual growth rates, the most likely effect of a 7 per cent fall in economic activity is for there to be an accompanying fall in the rate of economic growth. This comes about because businesses and households have a reduced capacity to save from their lower incomes. In turn, fewer funds are available for business to undertake investment which is the engine of economic growth. This explains why poor countries have a lower growth *potential* than do rich countries. Just what the reduction in the growth rate would have been consequent upon a 7 per cent reduction in work hours is uncertain because there are so many factors that might affect the outcome in one way or another. These factors include, but are not restricted to, the extent to which savings fall, changes in the rate of technical progress, changes in the level of natural resource productivity, changes in the birth rate, and the effect of increased leisure time on human capital development. It would give a false sense of precision if an attempt were made to quantify these factors.

Rather, we look here at two scenarios – one in which it is assumed that the growth rate would be 10 per cent lower; the other in which it is assumed that the growth rate is not affected. Regardless of the assumptions made, our primary purpose in undertaking this analysis is to show that reduced economic activity has a cumulative effect on the level of environmental degradation.

Scenario 1 (assumes annual growth rate falls by 10 per cent)

Since 1900, annual real GDP per capita growth in the US has been around 2 per cent. This growth caused real GDP per capita in the year 2000 to be about 7.25 times that in 1900. (*Real* GDP per capita growth tells us the rate at which the output of *goods and services* has grown. It ignores increases in the price level – inflation – that increase the money value of output even when the growth of output of goods and services is zero.) If increased leisure had reduced work effort and GDP per capita by 7 per cent in every one of those 100 years with an accompanying 10 per cent reduction in the overall growth rate bringing it down from 2 per cent per annum to 1.8 per cent per annum, then real GDP per capita in 2000 would have been only approximately 5.45 times that of 1900. In other words, if increased leisure had resulted in a 10 per cent reduction in per capita measured growth, GDP per capita in 2000 would have been about three quarters of its actual level (5.45/7.25). If this same reduction in work effort had occurred since 1800 and if per capita growth rates had been similar in the 19th century as in the 20th, per capita GDP in 2000 would have been less than two thirds of its actual level. As a result, the environment today would be far cleaner, many forests, fisheries, species and wilderness areas that have been lost would be intact and, most importantly, the QOL today would be significantly greater than it is – in spite of the lower level of measured GDP. It is interesting to observe that the GDP per capita that would have prevailed in the year 2000 if there had been a 10 per cent reduction in the growth rate as a result of reduced work effort every year over the previous 200 years is similar to the GDP per capita that prevailed in the mid-1970s when the GPI reached its peak

Scenario 2 (assumes annual growth rate unchanged)
If increased leisure had reduced work effort by 7 per cent in every year since 1900 but annual growth in GDP per capita had remained unchanged at 2 per cent per annum, then real GDP in 2000 would, in turn, have been 7 per cent less than its actual level in 2000. Rather than being approximately 7.25 times its actual level in 1900, it would have been approximately 6.75 times that level.

But knowing that real GDP per capita could have been 7 per cent (scenario 2) or 25 per cent (scenario 1) less today than it actually is tells only part of the story. The current state of the environment is not simply a function of current per capita economic activity; much of our environmental disamenity is the result of the accumulation of environmental damage that occurs year in and year out. There is, today, a very large amount of irreversible, or difficult to reverse, environmental damage that has been contributed to over the past 200 years as a result of excessive work hours. Some of this damage may be reversible at substantial cost to the community while some of it is irreversible. Panayotou cites examples of the crossing of critical ecological thresholds that irreversible damage involves. These include tropical deforestation, the loss of biological diversity, extinction of species, and destruction of fragile ecosystems and unique natural sites.[9]

It is also important to acknowledge that cumulative effects are not just applicable to the past. Excessive work, output and consumption that are occurring today are the basis of an excessive accumulation of environmental problems tomorrow.

Economic growth is usually thought of as the increase in future GDP, or GDP per capita, that results from the redirection of productive capacity away from consumption goods, which give present satisfaction, towards investment goods like factories, roads and computers that will increase future satisfaction by increasing output in the future. However, a decision by society to forgo growth in GDP per capita for the sake of the environment and the environmental amenity of future generations can, as Nobel prize-winning economist Robert Solow has pointed out, also be thought of as constituting economic growth.

Paradoxically, one of the ways in which the present can do something for the future is to conserve natural resources. If we get along with less lumber now so that there will be more forests standing for our grandchildren, or if we limit the present consumption of oil or zinc so that there will be some left for the 21st century, or if we worry about siltation behind dams that would otherwise be fun for fishermen and water-skiers, in all those cases we are promoting economic growth. I call that paradoxical because I think most people identify the conservation freak with the anti-growth party whereas, in this view of the matter, the conservationist is trading present satisfaction for future satisfaction, that is, he is promoting economic growth.[10]

Many readers may find it hard to accept that we would be better off if our current GDP per capita were significantly lower than it actually is. We probably cannot imagine having a lower income per capita than we experience today. Yet dissatisfaction with our QOL today is rife. The 1950s and 1960s (when measured GDP per capita was less than half what it is today) are often seen as a golden age, and studies of GPI suggest that QOL today is hardly changed from its level then. It should also be remembered that slower growth in GDP per capita does not necessarily mean that progress in science and technology or in human rights and politics would be slower. As Aristotle pointed out over 2000 years ago, increased leisure time spent in a benign environment may be conducive to great progress on these fronts. John Stuart Mill reminded us of this connection when he discussed the inevitable stationary state in which population growth and capital accumulation would cease.

> It is scarcely necessary to remark that a stationary condition of capital and population implies no stationary state of human improvement. There would be as much scope as ever for all kinds of mental culture, and moral and social progress; as much room for improving the Art of Living and much more likelihood of its being improved, when minds cease to be engrossed by the art of getting on.[11]

If doubt remains as to the benefits of more leisure and a lower GDP per capita, those who have experienced the horrendous pollution of large cities in rapidly developing countries might ask themselves if they would prefer even higher money incomes than they now have at the cost of being subjected indefinitely to pollution at these levels – to say nothing of the accompanying degradation of other environmental assets that is hidden from the casual visitor to these places. Alternatively, think of the most polluted residential area that you know of in your neighbourhood, be it close to an industrial estate or adjacent to a motorway. Would you be prepared to live permanently there in exchange for a higher income? If we are sure that we don't want to accept higher measured income at the cost of these higher levels of pollution, how sure can we be that we wouldn't prefer, in developed countries, to sacrifice some of today's income for a cleaner more sustainable environment?

WHAT IS TO BE DONE?

In relation to the extent of environmental degradation since the beginning of the industrial revolution, there is only so much that we can do. We can limit the continuing degradation as quickly as is prudent and, in the case of a limited range of degraded environmental assets, rehabilitate them if this can be done at a reasonable cost. The degradation that has already occurred and cannot be reversed – loss of species, destruction of old growth forests, contamination of soil, and so on – is what economists call a sunk cost – a cost that cannot be recovered. A homely example of a sunk cost is the cost of the return ticket that you buy to go from home to work and back on public transport. If, when you are at work, you are offered a ride home which will save you time and effort, it is rational to accept the ride and count the prepaid cost of the return journey as a sunk cost. Economic theory tells us that, save for their role in sometimes reminding us of our folly, we should ignore sunk costs in making decisions. And so it should be with these environment-related sunk costs. But, of course, we must accurately determine which costs are truly sunk and which are not, so that we can determine which to ignore. For example, we might choose not to incur the cost of recreating the dodo but decide that the restoration and reinstatement of wetlands, which has already occurred in some countries, is worth while. Economists have developed good tools for making these decisions. Longfellow gave wise counsel in this epitaph written more than a century ago.

> Look not mournfully into the Past. It comes not back again. Wisely improve the Present. It is thine. Go forth to meet the shadowy Future, without fear, and with a manly heart.[12]

The cumulative effect of the fundamental flaw has been with us since at least the commencement of the industrial revolution; and so has the practice of rich nations exploiting the resources of poor nations. Whereas, in colonial times, that exploitation emphasized both labour and natural resources, the contemporary relationship between developed and developing nations gives greater emphasis to exploitation of natural resources. Whether it be the rape of old growth forests, the despoliation of the countryside as a result of largely unregulated mining activities, or the pollution of cities that has accompanied the shift of manufacturing from the developed countries, many of the world's developing countries are characterized by large domestic environmental costs in relation to the levels of GDP per capita they produce. By contrast, the world's developed countries experience levels of domestic environmental cost that are smaller in relation to the levels of GDP per capita they produce. As we shall see shortly, the ecological footprints introduced in Chapter 2 can be used as an indication of the extent of these differences.

There are a number of reasons for these differences in relative environmental costs as between developed and developing countries. One reason is that, having long ago destroyed their stock of natural assets such as minerals and old growth forests, the world's developed countries have a limited capacity to impose further environmental costs on themselves. The environmental depletion that fuels their increased living standards must thus come from developing countries that have not yet proceeded so far down the road to ruin. A second reason, and one that is of particular interest to environmental economists, is the migration of polluting industries from developed countries to what are sometimes described as 'offshore havens' in developing countries. These havens for the developed world become hell for the developing countries that are willing to put up with horrendous levels of pollution and environmental disamenity for the sake of higher levels of measured GDP. In the next section we look at the way in which the unequal distribution of environmental costs between developed and developing countries affects the extent to which the fundamental flaw distorts the trade-off between work and leisure.

INTERNATIONAL DIFFERENCES IN THE FUNDAMENTAL FLAW

When the costs of the fundamental flaw were calculated in Chapter 5 it was revealed that environmental and congestion costs in the US amount to around 40 per cent of GDP. Subtraction of these costs from GDP leaves an EAI of 60 per cent of current GDP. The costs that are subtracted from GDP to obtain the EAI are those costs experienced by Americans in the domestic economy; but they do not constitute the total of the environmental costs that Americans impose on the world. The diversion of environmental costs from developed to developing countries means that Americans (and citizens of developed countries in general) are making calls on the environment of developing countries in addition to those incurred at home. If Americans were to experience at home the total of the environmental costs they impose on the world, their EAI would be significantly lower than the figure calculated on the basis of domestic environmental costs alone. Fortunately for them, however, a significant slice of these costs is transferred to developing countries like China from which much industrial production is imported. Commenting on China's environmental problems, Jared Diamond argues that not only are they are among the most severe of any major country but they are getting worse. His list of these problems includes 'air pollution, biodiversity losses, cropland losses, desertification, disappearing wetlands, grassland degradation, and increasing scale of and frequency of human-induced natural disasters, to [sic] invasive species, overgrazing, river flow cessation, salinization, soil erosion, trash accumulation, and water pollution and shortages.'[13]

An indication of the extent of the per capita transference of costs from the US to the rest of the world can be gained by looking at differences between the ecological footprint of the US and those of developing countries. In Chapter 2 it was explained that while the US has a per capita ecological footprint that is four times the world average, China's footprint is two-thirds of the world average while India's is just one-third. This means that the per capita footprint for the US is roughly six times that for China and 12 times that for India. In other words, for each person in the US, the call made on the world's biological productivity is approximately six times that made per person in China and 12 times that made per person in India. In Chapter 2 it was explained that a nation's call on the world's biological productivity can occur anywhere in the world. A major reason that countries like the US have lower domestic environmental costs per capita than do countries like China or India is that much of the world's natural resource-intensive production – especially manufacturing – is carried out in developing countries from where it is exported to the developed countries.

If developed countries encourage the location or relocation of natural resource-intensive and polluting industries to developing countries, this means that the environmental cost per dollar of GDP tends to fall in the developed countries and rise in the developing countries. Put another way, the EAI as a percentage of GDP per capita tends to rise in the developed countries and fall in the developing countries. The corollary to this is that the extent to which individuals work excessive hours as a result of the fundamental flaw is reduced in the developed countries and raised in the developing countries. This outcome is akin to the differences, discussed in Chapter 5, between the EAI in an individual country's congested and dirty urban areas as opposed to its cleaner and less congested rural areas.

As with our finding regarding differences in EAI as between high and low-income individuals that was discussed in Chapter 3, the implications of these differences between developed and developing countries are not likely to be seen in a favourable light. Just as we concluded in Chapter 3 that low-income earners are more subject to the fundamental flaw than are high-income earners and thus should reduce work hours by more than high-income earners, the lesson from our international comparisons is that workers in developing countries should make a greater reduction in their work hours than workers in developed countries.[14] Although, if such an outcome were to occur, it is likely to be seen as disadvantageous to citizens of developing countries, the reality is that these citizens should be measuring their well-being on the basis of QOL not on the basis of GDP. So long as any fall in GDP that accompanies shorter work hours results in a rise in QOL, the citizens of developing countries will be better off.[15] Indeed, shorter work hours might give them the opportunity to save elements of their natural environment that have already been sacrificed on the altar of progress in the developed nations. Although work-life balance is becoming something of a mantra in the developed world, the reality is that it may well be more of a problem in rapidly growing parts of the developing world.

PLEASURE, COMFORT AND FUTURE GENERATIONS

There is a saying that you don't miss what you never had. Acute observers are continually reminded of the nihilistic philosophical foundations of such a view of life as they witness the destruction of our heritage from generation to generation. Joni Mitchell's warning in the song *Big Yellow Taxi* 'that you don't know what you've got till it's gone' applies to the current generation; but future generations that are born into a world which has been despoiled by their forebears are none the wiser. Yet, well-being of a community is not a relative concept. It is absolute. We are not absolved of our obligations to future generations just because they will not know how much higher their QOL might have been if we had bequeathed them a better stock of environmental assets. We suffer a lower level of well-being – in spite of growth in measured GDP – than our parents experienced. If we do not mend our ways, our children's level of well-being will be even lower. This is the Easter Island effect that is so starkly revealed by anthropological studies into the role of environmental degradation in the near annihilation of Easter Island society in the middle of the second millennium.[16]

But what is it about human nature that allows this one-way street of environmental degradation to persist? The answer may lie in a distinction between *pleasure* and *comfort* that was introduced by Tibor Scitovsky and refined by fellow economist Albert Hirschman. In Hirschman's words, pleasure is the experience of travelling from discomfort to comfort while comfort is achieved at the point of arrival.[17] A state of continuing comfort robs us of the opportunity to experience pleasure. Hirschman argues that pleasure is the stuff of nondurable consumption while comfort comes from consumption of certain durables. Thus consumption of food gives great pleasure because it temporarily changes our state from one of discomfort to one of temporary satiation.[18] Similarly consumption of an entertaining film or concert may temporarily give great pleasure. As Hirschman points out '[t]here is something both pleasure-intensive and peculiarly disappointment-resistant about goods that disappear in consumption.'[19] On the other hand, says Hirschman, it is in the nature of durable goods such as an automatic heating system or a refrigerator to provide little pleasure. The continuity of the services provided by such goods means that we often take them for granted; they provide comfort but not pleasure. Now, if happiness is primarily a function of pleasure rather than comfort, consumption of the services of durables that maintain comfort will, according to Hirschman, disappoint in relation to consumption of nondurables that assuage discomfort.

Applying Hirschman's hypothesis to the environment, we can see that environmental amenity, which is the service produced by a durable good called the environment, is likely to provide comfort rather than pleasure. As is the case with durable consumption goods like refrigerators or washing machines we take the services that the environment provides for granted.

Thus we hardly notice the small marginal decline in the quality and quantity of these environmental services that continues inexorably from year to year, decade to decade and generation to generation. In rich countries the effect of this slow, inexorable decline is swamped by the pleasure afforded by every day consumption of a transitory nature. Only if a sudden and significant decline in the quality or quantity of environmental services were to occur would we experience a change in our comfort level. In this case the change would be the opposite of that explained by Scitovsky and Hirschman; it would involve a change from comfort to discomfort that brings about an intense feeling of *displeasure.* Minor and usually reversible examples of such changes include the devastation wrought by natural disasters such as floods, forest fires and hurricanes. A recent example of the displeasure that a sharp increase in global environmental disamenity might bring can be found in the desperate reaction to the oil crises of the 1970s which, at the time, were widely asserted to be the result of rapidly dwindling reserves of a non-renewable resource.

Until such time as the decline in the quality and quantity of the planet's environmental services is observed to be catastrophic, humanity will remain within its comfort zone from generation to generation oblivious to its ultimate fate. In the next chapter, policies designed to deal with the problem of the fundamental flaw are discussed in the context of a wide range of existing approaches to the problem of excessive environmental degradation.

The last word is given to John F. Kennedy:

> It is our task in our time and in our generation to hand down undiminished to those who come after us, as was handed down to us by those who went before, the natural wealth and beauty which is ours.[20]

NOTES

1   Keynes, J.M. (1938), 'Art and the State', in Williams-Ellis, C. (ed.), *Britain and the Beast*, London: Readers' Union, p. 1.
2   Keynes, J.M. (1938), 'Art and the State', in Williams-Ellis, C. (ed.), *Britain and the Beast*, London: Readers' Union, 1938, p. 2.
3   In some respects they were like indigenous communities before Western colonization. It is often said that these communities exercised a stewardship of nature that colonization destroyed . However, as Jared Diamond points out in his study of why some societies fail and some survive, not all indigenous communities have successfully practised sustainability. See Diamond, J. (2005), *Collapse*, Camberwell: Allen Lane.
4   Gordon, R.J. (2000), 'Does the New Economy Measure Up to the Great Inventions of the Past?', *Journal of Economic Perspectives*, **4** (14), p. 58.
5   Gordon, R.J. (2002). 'Two Centuries of Economic Growth: Europe Chasing the American Frontier, Economic History Workshop, Northwestern University, October, p. 18.
6   Cross, G. (1993), *Time and Money*, London: Routledge, p. 76.
7   See Thompson, E.P. (1963), *The Making of the English Working Class*, London: Penguin.

8   See, for example, Panatayou, T. (2000), 'Economic Growth and the Environment', *Centre for International Development Working Paper*, **56**, July.

9   Ibid., pp. 61–62.

10   Solow, Robert M. (1973), 'Is the End of the World at Hand?', *Challenge*, March-April, pp. 39–50, reprinted in part in Heilbroner, Robert L. and Ford, Arthur M. (1971), *Economic Relevance*, Pacific Palisades: Goodyear Publishing Company, p. 117.

11   Mill, J.S. (1871), *Principles of Political Economy*, vol. II, London: Longmans, Green, Reader and Dyer, pp. 330–2.

12   Longfellow, H.W. (2004), *Hyperion*, Project Gutenberg EBook, Ch. VIII at http://www.gutenberg.net/etext04/8hypr10.txt, accessed 18 July 2004.

13   See Diamond, J. (2005), p. 358.

14   This effect would be moderated to the extent that informed low-income-earning citizens of developing countries are willing to place a lower cost on any given level of environmental disamenity as compared to informed high-income-earning citizens of developed countries.

15   As is the case with income differences within a particular nation, this conclusion is subject to any adverse environmental effects that might be caused by a subsequent increase in income inequality between nations. See p.43 above.

16   Ponting, C. (no date), chapter excerpt from *A Green History of the World: The Environment and the Collapse of Great Civilizations* at http://www.primitivism.com /easter-island.htm, accessed 18 July 2004 and Diamond, J. (2005).

17   Hirschman, A. O. (1982), *Shifting Involvements*, Princeton, New Jersey: Princeton University Press, p. 27.

18   Ibid., pp. 28–29.

19   Ibid., p. 29.

20   Kennedy, John F. (1961), Speech dedicating the National Wildlife Federation Building, 3 March at http://www.stthomas.edu/recycle/future.htm , accessed 18 July 2004.

7. Policies to Tackle the Fundamental Flaw

One such cause [of the slow take-up of environmental taxes and other economic instruments] is the difficulty of putting into effective practice many of these mechanisms in a world of almost chaotic economic interrelationships and very incomplete knowledge of, for example, what polluting waste streams contain, where they come from and where they go, and what damage in the immediate and more distant future such emissions create.[1]

Timothy O'Riordan

The fundamental flaw in the capitalist system occurs primarily because of the existence of negative externalities that cause environmental harm to third parties who are not involved in the transactions that bring about this harm. The theme that is pursued in this book is that a significant reduction in the level of this harm can be effected by having workers work fewer hours in acknowledgement of the negative externalities that are generated by their work and consumption. By contrast, the policy approaches that have been pursued in the past have largely been directed at tackling each individual instance of negative externalities in a piecemeal fashion.

It was pointed out in Chapter 1 that the vast range of policies designed to deal with environmental harm has grown like Topsy as successive environmental problems have raised their ugly heads. The earliest of these policies were of a type described as involving 'command-and-control' instruments. These policies tackled the problems of environmental disamenity by directly prohibiting or limiting activities that caused them. Typical instruments of this type include specification of minimum sizes of fish or crustaceans that may be taken from open access fisheries, limits on the level of noise that may be emitted by producers and consumers, prohibitions or limits on emissions of air pollutants, and controls on logging of old growth forests.

With the increasing role of economics in the development of environmental policies, there has been very significant growth in the past three decades of an alternative approach involving what are described as 'economic instruments'. Economic instruments come in many forms. One of these forms involves taxes or charges on activities that cause environmental disamenity. Economists have developed principles that can guide policy-makers in designing instruments of this type that endeavour to bring about optimal reductions in the level of environmental damage. Another group of economic instruments is concerned with developing or changing property rights so as to give private ownership or control over resources such that the owner or controller has a vested interest in environmentally benign treatment of these resources. Examples of these instruments include the creation of transferable quotas for fisheries or for pollutants, and the development of conservation banks. Economists promote the use of these economic instruments, and, by and large, the business community supports them, because they are efficient and because they give greater autonomy (range of choices) to economic agents than do command-and-control instruments.

While there are important roles for both of these types of instruments in the modern array of piecemeal policies, a major theme of this book is that very significant benefits can flow from a more holistic approach.

HOLISTIC POLICY APPROACHES

The current approach to environmental policy that contains a mix of command-and-control and economic instruments involves an enormous range of mostly sensible, if not always optimal, policies that are directed at achieving a cleaner environment and a less stressful lifestyle. Later, it will be argued that these policies should form an important complement to a holistic policy of mandating reduced work time. In the meantime, however, we examine a range of holistic approaches that might substitute for, or complement, such a policy

The first holistic approach addressed is a government-sponsored public education campaign designed to discourage work effort.

A Public Education Programme

Governments are no strangers to public education campaigns. Whether they are designed to encourage safe motoring, safe sex, drinking in moderation, quitting the use of tobacco products, cleanliness, or good eating habits these campaigns are, to a greater or lesser degree, aimed at overcoming the effects of market failures. Indeed, there is a long history of governments being involved in work-time-related education campaigns. However, rather than discouraging work effort, these campaigns have usually encouraged increased work effort, particularly in times of war. Typically, these public education campaigns have, at war's end, been substituted by subtle campaigns designed to discourage women from work force participation so that demobilized males might have greater employment opportunities.

The excess work effort undertaken by citizens on account of the fundamental flaw is a clear case of a market failure caused by negative externalities – a market failure that economic theory tells us can be mitigated by government intervention. Not only is this market failure based on negative externalities, but it can also be thought of as involving an information failure that prevents ordinary citizens from even understanding that there is a link between their individual work effort and the level of environmental disamenity they experience. Thus an education campaign could be thought of as having two elements: 1) an awareness-raising element that explains the link between individual work effort and environmental disamenity; and 2) an element designed to change behaviour to reduce work effort. As we noted in Chapter 3, there is only so much that awareness-raising can achieve since individuals understand that a decision to act unilaterally to reduce work hours will, if their fellow citizens do not act in a similar fashion, have a negligible effect on the level of disamenity they experience. They are on a forced ride to somewhere they don't want to go. Nonetheless, it is possible that a combination of awareness-raising and encouragement to decrease work effort could have a significant effect.

In a sense, there is a public education programme already under way. This is evidenced by the burgeoning literature dealing with the causes of overwork and its effect on work-life balance. It is also manifested in the literature, perhaps best exemplified by Carl Honore's *In Praise of Slow*, that proactively encourages a more leisurely lifestyle.[2] It is doubtful, however, whether this literature on its own could seriously challenge the hold that consumerism has over individuals.

Without wanting to be too prescriptive about the nature of a public education campaign, it should be pointed out that such a campaign could be targeted at particular subgroups in the community or at the work force as a whole. Thus a campaign could encourage lower workforce participation by encouraging higher participation in tertiary education. Encouragement of increased involvement of men in family life could accompany a campaign to encourage lower male workforce participation; or, contrary to current trends based on the ageing of the population, earlier retirement could be encouraged in the way in which it once was in many countries. In relation to increased involvement of men in family life, Madeleine Bunting has remarked that 'the disinvestment of women in the caring [family] economy has not been accompanied by sufficient compensating investment by men.' The result, she says is 'a care deficit – a shortage of time and energy to invest in relationships.'[3]

While uncertainty as to the likely economic effectiveness of a public education campaign could be an impediment to its introduction, the reality is that the most important impediments to the introduction of public education campaigns are related more to political and sociological factors than they are to economic factors. Thus it is issues such as the political feasibility of openly discouraging work effort and the extent to which exhortation can override an ingrained work ethic that are likely to determine whether a public education campaign could play a role in mitigating the effects of the fundamental flaw. These are issues that are beyond the scope of this book.

Finally, it should be said that if a public education campaign were successful in encouraging a reduction in work effort, this approach to solving the problem of the fundamental flaw is likely to be looked upon favourably by economists. If availability of enhanced information about the problem results in voluntary corrective actions on the part of fully informed, sovereign economic agents then this is consistent with the mainstream economic paradigm.

Another possible holistic approach to the problems created by the fundamental flaw involves an economy-wide increase in the overall level of taxes. The propaganda that emphasizes the disincentive effects of taxation has been so pervasive and so persuasive that it is probable that an increase in the overall level of taxation in the economy would be seen by many as an obvious, if undesirable way of reducing work effort. The validity of such a view is discussed in the next section.

Increase Taxes

In all countries work effort is influenced by taxes on both incomes and consumption of goods and services. In developed countries national tax revenue is between 30 and 60 per cent of GDP. But what would be the effect on work effort of increases in tax revenue beyond current levels? We shall see that this depends on how QOL is affected by such an increase. In the discussion that follows an exceedingly broad brush approach will be taken. This approach largely ignores the widely understood differences in the effects of different taxes. These differences are dependent on factors such as the rate of tax, and the income or expenditure flows that are the basis for their collection. There can thus be very different outcomes from the levying of a tax depending, for example, on whether it is levied on personal income, corporate profits, consumption, imports, gifts and so on. There are also important differences in tax effects depending on whether the tax in question is levied at a single rate or at increasing or decreasing rates as, for example, expenditure or incomes rise. Although a more refined analysis must wait for another time, the discussion below identifies some broad principles that might give guidance as to whether an increase in the overall level of taxation would limit work effort and thus limit environmental damage and congestion.

The way in which taxes of all types affect work effort is a complex issue that has exercised the minds of economists in the public finance and labour economics areas for a very long time. Although justice cannot be done to the full range of relevant considerations here, there are some broad tendencies that can be addressed. It is important to keep in mind that throughout this analysis we are discussing the effects of an increase in the overall, or total, tax revenue of government across all tiers. It is also important to recognize that if governments balance their budgets over the long run, the overall level of taxes must equal the overall level of government outlays; any increase in the overall level of taxes must be accompanied by an equivalent increase in government expenditure.

The effect of an increase in taxes on work effort boils down to the relationship between the effect of the taxes in discouraging work effort through the substitution effect and the effect of the government expenditure financed by these taxes which might either discourage or encourage work effort through changes in QOL. The government expenditure effect will depend on the purposes to be fulfilled by this expenditure, and the way in which it affects the well-being of taxpayers. There are two possible outcomes that may occur as a result of an increase in taxes and the government expenditure they fund:

1. The increase in government expenditure made possible by increased taxes results in an increase in well-being as compared to a situation in which taxes and government expenditure remain unchanged. In other words, the rise in well-being caused by the increase in government expenditure is greater than the fall in well-being caused by the increase in taxes that funded it.
2. The increase in government expenditure made possible by increased taxes results in a decrease in well-being as compared to a situation in which taxes and government expenditure remain unchanged. In other words, the rise in well-being caused by the increase in government expenditure is less than the fall in well-being caused by the increase in taxes that funded it.

We look first at the case where increases in government expenditure financed by taxes raises well-being. In looking at this case, it is acknowledged that as well as instances where there is a self-interested view of the benefit of the tax payments, there are also cases where an altruistic motive is present.

Increased taxes raise well-being (case 1)
Contrary to popular perception, it is rational for taxpayers to self-interestedly consider that they are getting as much, or more, value for their money when governments spend their taxes on infrastructure or services as they would get from undertaking an equivalent amount of private expenditure themselves. That is, they believe that governments can spend part of their personal income in a way that would increase their well-being more than if they spent the income themselves. An everyday example might be government expenditure on a police force that would reduce the likelihood of our being victims of crime to a greater extent than would be the case if we spent the money ourselves on our own private security measures. An example relating to the environment might be a government-funded programme to develop parkland that has better outcomes than would an equivalent amount of expenditure undertaken by individuals in an attempt to provide their own

green space in individual housing lots. The efficacy of state expenditure in these examples stems, at least in part, from their having a strong public good element – an element that was described in Chapter 2 as involving a market failure that causes less than optimum production levels in the private sector.

Taxpayers will also self-interestedly support taxes that fund some redistributive measures. They may see them as providing insurance against a possible future need to call upon these redistributive measures themselves.[4] They may also consider that they would suffer less from crime and antisocial behaviour if there was a more egalitarian distribution of income. However, rather than being motivated solely by these self-interested considerations, taxpayers may also support such redistributive measures in an altruistic way, expecting to obtain no direct benefit themselves but, nonetheless, experiencing an improvement in their own QOL by improving that of others.

Regardless of the taxpayers' motivation for a belief that they are getting as much, if not more, value for money from the taxes they pay than they would get from spending the money themselves, under these conditions an increase in taxes is likely to cause workers to work fewer hours for two reasons. First, the increased tax discourages work effort as workers substitute leisure for the now less well remunerated work. Second, because the government expenditure that is funded by these taxes has the effect of raising QOL (by more than if the taxpayer had undertaken the expenditure themselves), taxpayers reduce their work effort because they now require less work-based money income to achieve a given level of happiness. In the language we developed in Chapter 2, the substitution and income effects are both discouraging work effort. In addition to this, if redistributive government expenditure (welfare payments) increase and this also discourages work effort on the part of its recipients then the overall discouragement effect is increased. In short, increases in government taxation and expenditure that raise QOL discourage work effort. Next we look at the case where an increase in government expenditure funded by an overall increase in the level of tax revenue reduces well-being.

Increased taxes reduce well-being (case 2)
If, on the other hand, taxpayers find that increases in taxation unequivocally reduce their well-being, the effect of increased taxes may, contrary to the assertions of business, be to increase work effort. As in the previous case, the increased taxes will discourage work effort as leisure is substituted for the now lower paid work. However, unlike the previous case, the fall in QOL that results from the government spending its tax proceeds in a way that gives less value for money than if the taxpayers had undertaken the expenditure themselves means that taxpayers will increase their work effort. In the language developed in Chapter 2, the substitution effect is discouraging work effort while the income effect is encouraging it. The net effect will depend on the relative strength of these two forces – as well as any discouragement

effect related to welfare payments financed by increased taxation. If, in this case, a decision to increase taxes and government expenditures from their current levels has the effect of lowering QOL to such an extent that the encouragement to increase work effort dominates, such a decision will result in an overall increase in work effort.

The foregoing discussion of the possible effects of tax increases suggests that they can either increase or decrease well-being. We shall see that this implies that there is an optimum overall level of taxes.

The optimum level of taxes

Governments in democratic capitalist societies tax and spend at the behest of the electorate in order to raise the well-being of the community. The fundamental justification for taxation is that by spending individuals' incomes on their behalf they can raise well-being by more than if those individuals were to undertake that expenditure themselves. If a zero tax regime was what maximized our well-being we could reasonably expect democracies to have this outcome. However, they do not.

Even economists who champion laissez-faire such as the founder of modern economics, Adam Smith, or libertarian, Milton Friedman, have argued for a positive level of taxes to fund the minimal level of government expenditure that they consider to be justified. Thus, from their point of view, taxes that fund the legislature, the judicial system, the police force, the defence force, elementary education and other such unavoidable essentials to a functioning capitalist society raise welfare above the level that would prevail if such taxes were not levied and if such expenditures were not to occur. They argue that the community is made better off because this government expenditure raises well-being by more than if the expenditure were to be undertaken by individuals themselves.

In contrast to the manifestos of libertarian economists, the electorates of modern capitalist nations have indicated that their preference is for much higher levels of taxation and government expenditure than would provide for the unavoidable essentials for a functioning capitalist society. This additional government expenditure is seen as providing a greater increment to well-being than if private individuals had not paid the enabling taxes but had undertaken the expenditure themselves. Nonetheless, there must come a stage where government taxation and spending has risen to a level beyond which an increase in taxes and government spending would add less to community well-being than would occur if private individuals undertook this expenditure themselves. Although a regime of very high levels of taxes and accompanying government expenditure may sensibly characterize a democratic nation at war, no democratic society would maximize its well-being by confiscating all of its citizens' income for the purpose of undertaking government expenditure. There is thus an optimal level of taxes that lies somewhere between 0 per cent and 100 per cent of national income.

Of course, many individuals would prefer that all of their fellow citizens continued to make their contributions to the taxes that fund worthwhile government spending while they paid no taxes at all. In short, they would be happy to free-ride on the contributions of their fellow citizens. If all citizens attempted to do so and were successful, well-being would fall to the level that would prevail if no taxes were levied in the first place; anarchy may prevail. Thus we have the logic of collective action that says that we will all be better off if we can all agree to participate in certain courses of action, using coercion by the democratically elected government to prevent free-riding if necessary.

It can be inferred from the foregoing discussion that the optimal level of overall taxation arises where taxes are raised to such a level that additional taxing and spending by the government would reduce well-being. Obviously, achievement of the optimal level of taxing and spending by government involves it in a process of iterative testing over the long term as it gropes for the outcome that will maximize the well-being of the community. Nonetheless, it is assumed here that the current level of taxing and spending in democratic nations is at or near the optimal level.[5] Thus, contrary to the opinions of conservatives who argue that taxes are too high, the position taken here is that, through democratic processes, citizens have chosen of their own free will the level of taxes that currently prevails. How else can we explain the increase in government spending (and the taxation and government charges that funds it) in the US from less than 4 per cent of GDP in the last quarter of the 19th century to over 30 per cent in the last quarter of the 20th century?[6] The magnitude of this increase conforms to a pattern found in all modern democracies. It seems hard to believe that, over the past 100 years, increasingly informed and enfranchised communities in these countries would have chosen to suffer a development such as this if it were inimical to their well-being.[7] It is this principle that underlies the assertions of some economists to the effect that levels of taxing and spending in capitalist countries may be optimal. Perhaps the most prominent of the papers dealing with this topic is economist Donald Wittman's 'Why Democracies Produce Efficient Results' published in the prestigious *Journal of Political Economy*.[8]

There is, however, a proviso to the assumption that the current level of aggregate taxes is at or near the optimum. It is that this optimum prevails in a world where individuals, who are ignorant of the effects of the fundamental flaw in reducing the reward from their work effort, are duped into working excessively long hours. In other words, the levels of taxing (and spending) in developed countries are based on levels of GDP per capita that are, because of the fundamental flaw, in excess of those that should prevail. This means that current aggregate levels of taxing and spending are likely to be greater than would be optimal if GDP were to decline as a result of a reduction in work hours consequent upon acknowledgement of the fundamental flaw.

A move to a lower level of GDP as a result of an understanding that the fundamental flaw is causing us to work excessively long hours is thus likely to require a concomitant fall in the overall level of tax revenue collected by government. But, of course, government will have less reason to undertake expenditure if there are fewer environmental and work-life balance problems that require amelioration.

An understanding that current levels of taxation may be optimal is perhaps the most important point to be got across to politicians, policy-makers and the electorate who have been subjected to relentless propaganda from the anti-tax lobby which, by downplaying the purposes to which tax revenue is put, argues that increased taxes always lead to reduced work effort because they reduce personal disposable money income. Another factor which can result in misleading interpretations of the effects of tax changes is the difference in the time taken for individuals to recognize and act on the cause of the substitution effect as opposed to the cause of the QOL effect. Whereas a reduction in the purchasing power of salary and wages caused by a tax increase is felt immediately, the change in QOL that is brought about by the expenditure of this increased tax revenue may take months or years to be realized.

Notwithstanding our argument to the effect that an increase in taxes is unlikely to be an appropriate policy to tackle the fundamental flaw, it remains that if an increase in the overall level of taxes would move society closer to an optimum that it has not yet achieved, then such an increase may be appropriate. For those sceptics who may find it hard to believe that taxpayers could even contemplate the idea that their well-being might be increased by a rise in taxes, the following quote from Professor of European Studies, Tony Judt, contains a salutary lesson.

> Europeans want a more interventionist state at home than Americans do, and they expect to pay for it. Even in post-Thatcher Britain, 62 per cent of adults polled in December 2002 would favour higher taxes in return for improved public services. The figure for the US was under 1 per cent. This is less surprising when one considers that in America (where the disparities between rich and poor are greater than any where else in the developed world) fully 19 per cent of the adult population claims to be in the richest 1 per cent of the nation – and a further 20 per cent believe they will enter that 1 per cent in their lifetime![9]

The vast difference in the views of Europeans and Americans serves to bring home the point that perceptions and reality can be very different. Although Americans may not perceive that higher taxes would raise their well-being, the reality may be that they would.

Finally, it should be noted that taxation that *does* have the effect of reducing work effort in the work place may at the same time encourage home-based work activities. That is, the increased 'leisure' that may be the result of increased taxation is likely to be devoted, at least in part, to home-based production. Put simply, if tax imposts mean that less effort is required to produce a good or service at home rather than earn the income with which it may be bought in the market place, then home-based production will be encouraged. In Chapter 2, it was explained that home-based work activities are much less likely to cause negative externalities than do work-based activities. To the extent that this is the case, any tax-induced transfer of work from the work place to the home will be environmentally beneficial.

So much for the complexities of the role that a holistic policy of increased taxes might play in reducing environmental disamenity; in the next section we return to the piecemeal policies that we have said will have an important complementary role alongside shorter work hours. We commence by looking at the range of existing policies designed to mitigate the effects of negative externalities.

PRICE-IN OR TAX THE NEGATIVE EXTERNALITIES

As we saw in Chapter 2, when an act of production or consumption causes a negative externality, the party responsible for that act imposes a cost on other members of society. If institutional arrangements were such that the party responsible for the negative externality was required to make payment to the affected members of society, and such payment was actually made, we would say that the externality had been internalized. Even where institutional arrangements that would facilitate payment to a third party cannot be made, or would be too costly to implement, the wide powers of governments to impose taxes and levies can sometimes result in imposition of a tax or levy that is equivalent to the cost imposed by the originator of the externality. Whether it is the result of institutional change or as a result of the introduction of a tax or levy, the imposition of additional costs on the producer or consumer means that the level of the externality-creating activity will decline. An example of a tax that diminishes certain negative externalities, but certainly does not eliminate them, is the tax on petrol. Taxes designed to internalize externalities are often described by economists as corrective taxes.

Consistent with this approach, a *positive* externality would be internalized if those who benefit from positive externalities were to make payment to the originator. If such payment could not be readily procured, a similar outcome could be achieved by government paying a subsidy to the originator. In this case the additional payment to the producer or consumer would mean that the externality-creating activity would increase. An example of a subsidy for a positive externality-creating activity is the support given by many governments to medical research. As we saw in Chapter 3, there will be many fewer positive externalities than negative externalities, primarily because the profit motive promotes the capture of revenue that accompanies internalization of positive externalities, and the shifting of costs to third parties that is enabled by negative externalities. In the remainder of this section we concentrate on negative externalities which are the root cause of the fundamental flaw.

If all negative externalities could be internalized or appropriately taxed, the problem of excessive environmental damage and disamenity would no longer exist. This is the rationale that underpins the general approach to this problem that has been increasingly pursued by economists and policy-makers in recent years. The environmental economics literature abounds with examples of environmental taxes and levies, and proposals for the creation of property rights that are designed to reduce negative externalities. Furthermore, environmental taxes are increasingly supported by environmentalists who, although they may not necessarily look favourably upon economics as a discipline, see the benefits of such an approach. Hazel Henderson, a sensitive and informed critic of the economic paradigm, explains the advantages of pricing-in the externalities:

> To move forward and achieve these goals [of sustainability and even environmental enhancement and restoration], there already is a wide consensus among economists and environmentalists that we must, as soon as possible and by a range of appropriate means, move to full-cost pricing, i.e., internalise as quickly as possible all the longer-term social and environmental costs of production back onto the company balance sheets, so that the products and services may be truly priced.[10]

In relation to taxation of negative externalities, business typically greets such proposals with dire warnings that the disincentive effects of the taxes will reduce economic activity. As we saw when we discussed the effects of increased taxes, they may or may not be right about the fall in the level of economic activity; but, if it should eventuate, they are certainly wrong to warn us against it. In this context, less economic activity means more leisure time and a cleaner environment – in short, an increase in our well-being. The practical problem, of course, is that the increased leisure that these taxes may encourage could well be manifested as forced leisure in the form of unemployment – unemployment that will adversely affect some areas of the economy more than others. As we shall see later in this chapter, achievement of increased leisure through a mandated decrease in work hours would be less discriminatory and involve less dislocation in the economy than would the universal application of taxes on negative externalities. The theoretical justification for economic instruments that price-in or tax negative externalities is incontrovertible; however, as we shall see in the next section, the case for their practical application is less clear cut.

LIMITATIONS TO THE EFFECTIVENESS OF CURRENT INSTRUMENTS

The reality is that these instruments cannot deal with all the negative externalities that occur; and those that can be successfully employed may take a long time to be effective. They are examples of the ad hoc, 'symptoms rather than causes' approach that was criticized in Chapter 1. While this approach should continue to be pursued, it is clear that, as is the case with health issues, a more holistic approach – akin to, say, health education or immunization – is required. Such an approach will attack the problem at its source rather than waiting for the QOL-destroying environmental disamenity to rear its ugly head and do enormous damage while we wait for the policy 'cure' to be implemented and take effect.

Moreover, for political reasons, there may be many instances where a policy cure is just not possible. Examples abound of environmental problems that have not been nipped in the bud and which are now either very difficult to correct or are unable to be corrected at all. An example is the use of SUVs which, in addition to their gas-guzzling behaviour on the road network, do untold damage to environmental assets such as soils, forests, sand dunes and beaches. Had policy-makers foreseen this potential for damage, it is unlikely that the current freedom to use these vehicles in many environmentally sensitive locations would have been granted. But now the voter considers it a right rather than a privilege to use their vehicles in these areas.

Think of the damage to the ozone layer caused by CFCs. It was only when the extent of the damage was finally recognized and an international agreement put in place that their use was curtailed. But in the meantime significant environmental damage was caused. On the other hand, if we had been taking more leisure over the past centuries, money incomes and wealth would currently be far lower, and the use of SUVs and CFCs would be far lower. However, in spite of the lower money incomes and wealth, as we have demonstrated, QOL would be far higher.

No policy can recreate extinct species but if we had been following the holistic approach involving the substitution of leisure for work, far fewer species would be extinct today.[11] This argument becomes even more persuasive when we consider the limited assimilative capacity of the environment.[12] At low levels of environmental damage, sustainability can be achieved because the environment has the capacity to correct this damage through natural processes. Thus pollution can be cleansed by the system, and the damage to forests, fisheries, and wildlife can be mitigated as a result of natural rehabilitation. A decision to choose more leisure and less work would mean that we are less likely to come up against these limits to the assimilative capacity of the environment.

Another disadvantage of the piecemeal approach to policy is that many of the instruments employed involve high administration and monitoring costs.

Thus, for example, economic instruments such as taxes on pollution or creation of quotas to pollute require the agency which is implementing policy to incur the costs of continually measuring levels of pollution to ensure compliance.[13] Similarly, command-and-control instruments that prohibit or place physical limits on certain activities must also be administered and policed at a significant cost to the community.

Having pointed out some of the advantages of a policy approach that promotes increased leisure as opposed to one that uses ad hoc policies involving taxation of negative externalities, it is important to acknowledge a particular advantage that these ad hoc policies have. This is their capacity to discourage environmentally damaging activities and, at the same time, *encourage environmentally benign activities*. A simple example is the best way to explain this outcome. Imagine that it is politically feasible to increase taxes on motor cars, petrol and tyres so that they reflect the full costs that motoring imposes on the environment – both when motoring goods are produced and when they are consumed. Furthermore, imagine that congestion charges are levied to reflect the costs imposed on other motorists by crowding the roads. These taxes and charges would raise the overall costs of motoring considerably. The outcome would be for individuals to consume fewer motoring goods and services – either by driving less or by substituting smaller, more fuel efficient vehicles or, more likely, by a combination of both. If, at the same time, production and consumption of goods and services used in environmentally benign activities such as web-browsing or cycling were untaxed, consumers would increase their consumption of these goods and services. Put simply, a rise in the price of motoring relative to browsing or cycling would encourage substitution of browsing and cycling for motoring. Environment-friendly consumption is substituted for damaging consumption. This is part of the so-called 'green tax' agenda that we alluded to previously. It has many advocates. In its simplest form this policy approach involves abolishing existing taxes on environmentally neutral or benign activities and replacing them with new or increased taxes on environmentally damaging activities.

Clearly there is an important place for policies that discourage environmentally damaging consumption and production activities. However, the limitations to their applicability brought about by political exigencies, the typically long lags that occur between recognition of the extent of damage to the environment and its amelioration, and the absence of global institutions to deal with environmental damage that crosses national boundaries mean that a more holistic approach involving less work and more leisure should be the centrepiece of our policy approach.

Returning to the health analogy, it is better to provide treatment for specific health problems when they intrude into our healthy lifestyle rather than allow citizens to lead an unhealthy lifestyle that spawns a large number of specific health problems requiring continual treatment.

So, if a shorter working week is the best way of achieving the environmental outcomes and quality of life we desire, how do we achieve this end? Can we harness the union movement?

HARNESSING THE UNION MOVEMENT

In developed countries and in many developing countries, unions have an important role to play in determining the rates of pay of workers and the terms and conditions of their employment. It was the union movement that played a pivotal role in the achievement of the eight-hour day. In recent times, however, the union movement has given less emphasis to advocacy of reduced working hours than it did in the first half of the 20th century when hours of work were reduced by approximately one-third. There are, however, some recent exceptions. In many European countries, including France and Germany, the union movement has successfully agitated for shorter work hours.[14] In Australia the union movement has recently made a case for a shorter working week. More generally, unions in most developed countries have been calling for more family-friendly work practices that give employees greater flexibility, self-imposed limits to hours worked, and paid parental leave.

A reading of the cases put forward by unions for family-friendly work practices and reduced working hours indicates that they are very much aware of the decline in QOL that accompanies long working hours. The union movement is also acutely aware of the environmental problems that we face. Typically, however, the union perspective is not based on the liberal economic tradition but rather, on some variant of democratic socialism. The arguments in this book are thus not likely to strike a chord with the union movement. The idea that we should work fewer hours per week is, of course, acceptable; the idea that we should be happy with a lower weekly money wage is not. The union movement typically wants fewer hours for the same pay. While this may be achievable in the short term — and in the long term if worker productivity rises or if inflation eats away at the purchasing power of workers' pay leaving them with an effectively reduced income – it is an unavoidable consequence of the approach developed here that reduced working hours will be accompanied by reduced money incomes. But, as we have seen, the rise in QOL will more than offset the decline in money income leaving us with a higher level of well-being. This is the message that must be got through to the union movement if their support for significant reductions in the working week is to be harnessed. Recall that in Chapter 2 it was argued that the claim that shorter working hours would raise productivity to such an extent that no decrease in pay would be warranted is a claim that reduced working hours do not reduce output. This is not the outcome that we are looking for; the major objective is to reduce our call on the environment by reducing output and consumption. Nonetheless, if support from the union movement for shorter hours with reduced pay were forthcoming, this could assist greatly in the successful implementation of the previously discussed policy of instituting a public education campaign. It would also assist with achievement of a goal of mandated shorter work hours which is discussed in the next section.

An interesting development in Australia which does involve reduced pay for reduced work hours is the offering of the opportunity for employees to purchase leave. Australia's peak union body, the ACTU, supports this development which has been offered to employees by a number of government departments and agencies, and by a small number of universities and businesses. The idea is that employees may elect to purchase so-called short-term leave by increasing the number of weeks of annual vacation they take. Their annual salary is reduced accordingly but in order to minimize the adverse impact of this reduction, a lower weekly wage is paid for each week of the year – including the vacation weeks. Alternatively, employees may opt for long-term purchased leave involving one year off in every five years with employees being paid four fifths of their usual salary for every year including the one that they have off. In effect, the opportunity to 'purchase' leave extends the possibilities for part-time work beyond the common practice of working for part of the week to include work for part of the year or part of a five-year period.[15]

Unfortunately, in spite of the widespread acknowledgement of the benefits of additional time for care of children during school vacations, care of the elderly, civic engagement and study, the take-up rate of purchased leave has been disappointingly low. Although this outcome may be consistent with the idea, presented in Chapter 2, that the existing level of work effort in contemporary society accurately reflects the preferences of employees, our knowledge of the fundamental flaw indicates that this outcome is, however, not consistent with maximization of employees' well-being; the negative externalities that dupe us into working excessive hours prevent us from choosing to extend our unpaid leisure time through schemes such as purchased leave.

As with other areas of market failure, it seems that government may have to mandate the outcomes that will maximize our well-being.

MANDATED SHORTER WORKING HOURS

Governments do a lot of mandating. Whether it is opening hours for bars and bottle shops, the fuel efficiency of motor cars, the zoning of urban land for different uses, or compulsory education, the controlling hand of the state is a prominent, though often unacknowledged, feature of contemporary liberal democracies. In these countries the state also mandates monogamy and requires that we cover certain parts of our bodies in public.[16] It can even be argued that the state has mandated the free enterprise system by legislating for, and encouraging, the institutions of capitalism. Madeleine Bunting quotes John Gray's argument that whereas modern capitalism is based on 'the theory that market freedoms are natural and political restraints on markets are artificial, [t]he truth is that free markets are creatures of state power, and persist only so long as the state is able to prevent human needs for security and the control of economic risk from finding political expression.'[17]

Mandated shorter working hours would suit many individuals. More leisure time and a more leisurely pace on the consumption treadmill are likely to be embraced wholeheartedly by most workers – but only if wages are not reduced. Unfortunately, as we saw when we discussed harnessing the unions, the economy has little capacity to pay higher rates per hour when there is a decrease in hours worked.

Yet, a reduction in hours worked that is accompanied by an approximately proportionally lower wage has been demonstrated in the previous chapters to actually raise well-being. So how can we achieve this? Our current leaders and their predecessors have had no shortage of opportunities to learn how to mandate behaviour in cases where the electorate sees the mandated behaviour as not being in their best interest. Examples include compulsory education which was vehemently opposed by many parents including farmers concerned about the loss of family labour, fluoridation of water that has been opposed by both conservatives and progressives alike, and conscription that has occurred in many countries in times of war.

Although economists generally favour economic instruments for regulation of environmentally harmful activities, they are nonetheless aware that mandating – a command-and-control approach – can in many instances achieve desired ends more efficiently. Thus, for example, lead-free petrol is mandated, as is the absence of asbestos in building products. Mandating occurs because the ill-effects of these substances on human health are large, irreversible and unacceptable. A similar case can be argued for mandating work hours.

What is required is a political campaign directed at a mandated reduction in work hours accompanied by a reduction in wages. Lest this be thought to be inconsistent with the liberal economic approach, it should be pointed out that the liberal approach supports government intervention where market failure occurs; and, as has been demonstrated, excessive work hours brought about because externalities are not taken into account is a prime example of market failure. Commenting that supporting government through a tax system is a dilemma of collective action that requires, for its success, a commitment from citizens not to free-ride on the goodwill of others, Robert Putnam argues that in this case, and others like it, the solution lies in '…an institutional mechanism with the power to ensure compliance with the collectively desirable behaviour.'[18] Mandating work hours is such an institutional mechanism. It is one *that is used already* in most liberal democracies alongside far less contentious examples of mandating such as compulsory registration of births and deaths, compulsory immunization, prohibition of recreational drug use and regulation of road safety. As in the cases of compulsory education, fluoridation of water, and conscription, a public education programme would need to accompany a political campaign for mandated shorter work hours. Bipartisan or multipartisan support for the reduced working week would also be of great benefit in achieving acceptance of the change.

Robert Gordon of Northwestern University notes that it is well known that in Europe, '...postwar governments have encouraged (and/or labor unions have demanded) longer vacations, contributing to the decline in hours per employee...' He goes on to point out, as we saw in Chapter 3, that '[t]o the extent that Europe's standard of living (measured by its relative output per capita) is held down by lower hours due to longer vacations, then its citizens have chosen to use some of their prosperity to take longer vacations in contrast to the overworked American.' Neglecting the market failure argument, he then goes on to question the validity of this outcome, asking whether Europeans have really chosen such long vacations voluntarily or whether this outcome could be '...the result of union or parliamentary politics.'[19] Contrary to this position, it has been argued here that the fundamental flaw is, indeed, a market failure that requires government or union intervention to correct it.

In relation to a decision to mandate shorter work hours, an important question that arises is whether employees would endeavour to compensate for the effect of these shorter work hours by seeking increased overtime in their usual work place or by taking on extra part-time jobs. This also raises the issue of small business proprietors and the self-employed; can they somehow be encouraged to put in a shorter work hours? In relation to small business proprietors and the self-employed, if the great majority of workers are working shorter hours it is likely that they will do so as well. They may simply fall into line with their employees, clients and suppliers who are working shorter hours; alternatively their direct observation of the benefits gained by employees who work shorter hours may encourage them to do likewise. In relation to workers choosing to work overtime or take on extra jobs, this demonstration effect may also be important. Nonetheless, it may be more difficult to bring about a reduction in work hours for small business proprietors and the self-employed than it would be for employees.

There are many ways in which a mandated decrease in working hours could be achieved – and there is no need for a one-size-fits-all policy. The authors of *Affluenza* suggest that the US average of around 2000 working hours per year could be reduced to around 1500 hours which is typical for European nations. This could be done by reduction in days worked per week or hours worked per day or some combination of both.[20] However, a reduction in weekly work hours is but one, albeit the most important, way of reducing work effort. Other ways in which work hours may be reduced include increased holidays and vacations, fewer working years within a lifetime, and provision of more opportunities for part-time work. We look briefly at these in the following sections.

More Public (National) Holidays and Longer Annual Vacations

Sharon Beder in her *Selling the Work Effort* points out that the rise of Protestantism in Europe was fuelled by the desire of the commercial classes to dispense with the plethora of Catholic holy days and saints' days that reduced work time and ate into their profits.[21] Now it is time to reverse the trend − but the community need not promote Catholicism to achieve its aim. In our largely secular societies, governments could embark on a programme of increasing the number of public holidays. In the last half of a century almost no additional public holidays have been declared in the developed world. As with many of the policy proposals presented here, a solution must be found to the question of how the support of the business lobby might be achieved. A similar solution would need to be found to the problem of opposition to a policy of increasing the length of annual vacations.

The length of annual vacations varies considerably around the world. In the US − the country with the highest GDP per capita in the world − the norm is two weeks. In Australia which has struggled to stay in the top 20 in terms of GDP per capita, workers have four weeks annual leave. When expressed in percentage terms the comparison is stark. Americans' annual holidays take up 3.85 per cent of the weeks of the year; Australians' take up 7.7 per cent. If Australians can do it on their lower money incomes why can't Americans?

The answer probably lies in the fact that whereas in Australia, as in most of Europe, the length of vacations is now statutorily determined, in America it is part of the labour contract. 'The American worker's vacation was not to be an entitlement of citizenship but a privilege, rewarding loyal service at work in the most organised sectors of the economy (government and big business).'[22] Mandating a longer duration of annual vacations in the US is an obvious way to reduce work time.

Fewer Years of Work

In Chapter 2 it was noted that over the last century there has been a huge reduction in the proportion of our lifetime waking hours that are spent at work. This has come about for two main reasons. First, factors such as early retirement and increased participation rates in higher-level education have reduced the absolute number of years in the workforce. Second, large increases in life expectancy have greatly increased our lifetime waking hours. The ways in which the absolute number of years spent in the workforce could be reduced are many and varied. They include even more years of education, significant periods of absence from the workforce between career commencement and retirement, and earlier retirement. In relation to earlier retirement, the attempts by many governments to solve the perceived problems of a greying population by using sticks and carrots to get older people to remain in the workforce so they are less of a burden on taxpayers is an unfortunate development that will result in more output and consumption, more congestion and greater environmental degradation. The blinkered thinking of the politicians, bureaucrats and academics who give no consideration to the broader environmental consequences of their policy proposals means that these adverse environmental effects are ignored completely.

The number of years spent at work is related to the workforce participation rate of the individual; that is, it is related to the degree to which the individual chooses to be in the workforce as opposed to being voluntarily unemployed. A rise in the participation rate for any given cohort of workers results in more output, more income, more consumption, and more environmental degradation. A big contributor to increased production and consumption over the past three decades has been the increased participation of women in the workforce.[23] As was noted above, this has, according to Madeleine Bunting, led to a care deficit in the home because women's increased participation has not been offset to any significant extent by lower participation rates for men. Any opportunity to decrease participation rates – particularly those of men – is an opportunity to make good the care deficit and increase environmental amenity. Similar benefits would flow from increased opportunities to substitute part-time work for full-time work.

Provide More Opportunities for Part-time Work

As many commentators have pointed out, not everyone wants a part-time job but many people do. The benefit to society of substitution of part-time for full-time work accrues not only in less congestion and environmental disamenity but also, as Robert Putnam has pointed out, in the form of more civic engagement. Putnam and his researchers found that part-time workers are generally more involved in community activities than are full-time workers or those who are not employed at all.[24] More generally, we might expect that an overall reduction in work hours in almost any form would increase the propensity for citizens to become civically engaged.

Clearly, there are many ways in which a reduced work effort could be mandated. Each will have advantages and disadvantages – both in relation to their efficacy and in relation to their political feasibility. It is also important to understand that each of the many ways of reducing work effort is interrelated; this means that a policy of mandating shorter work hours must safeguard against a reduction of work effort in one domain leading to an increase in another. So, for example, a policy that reduces hours worked each week might be ineffective if, as a consequence, workers are able to compensate for this by extending their retirement age.

IF ALL ELSE FAILS …

Reductions in working time over the long haul notwithstanding, it is clear from the discussion in Chapter 5 that the degree of sensitivity of work hours to changes in remuneration is very low. Taken with the effect of declining QOL in encouraging work effort, this may suggest some difficulty with finding policies that would decrease this effort. If significant decreases in work effort cannot be achieved what can be done? A logical, but perhaps not obvious solution suggested by the analysis undertaken in this book would be to encourage activities that generate positive externalities.[25] This would mean, in effect, tailoring our productive activities to our work effort rather than the other way around.[26] Recall that in our introductory discussion of the role of positive externalities in Chapter 3 it was pointed out that if, in an imaginary world, the only externalities that existed were positive externalities, the amount of work undertaken would be suboptimal. In deciding on the level of our work effort we would fail to include the external benefits it generated. Under such conditions, optimality would be achieved by workers *increasing* their work effort.

As was also pointed out in Chapter 3, the capacity of economic agents to internalize the benefits from activities that might otherwise generate positive externalities while externalizing costs wherever possible has led to a situation in contemporary economies in which the costs of negative externalities swamp the benefits of positive externalities. While this suggests that an increase in activities that generate positive externalities might not occur spontaneously, it is, nonetheless, the case that encouragement by the state of such activities could increase their level significantly. On the assumption that the positive externalities so generated would not be lost as a result of capture by a small number of individual economic agents but would, rather, be widely dispersed, this would result in a decrease in the extent to which current work effort in contemporary market economies is excessive.

There is a large range of activities that could potentially generate positive externalities. They include restoration of degraded environmental assets such as wetlands, fisheries and forests, development of gene banks, enhancement of police services, and the fostering of civic engagement. By and large, encouragement of these activities would require intervention and subsidization by the state.

Finally, we have seen that there is a multitude of ways in which work effort might be reduced including a public education campaign and mandating shorter work hours. In this chapter emphasis has been given to mandating shorter work hours; and fortunately, when it comes to assessing the likely success of such a policy we have history on our side. In the West, the duration of the working day, the working week, the working year and the working life have all fallen dramatically over the past century. By and large, the initiation of these reductions has been accompanied by statutory measures. The power of the state has been used to fulfil the aspirations of workers. Nonetheless, because of the ubiquity of the fundamental flaw, these aspirations have fallen short of what is required for the optimization of our well-being.

As the discussion above suggests, mandating shorter hours should, as a policy, be accompanied by a range of supplementary policies many of which are already in place to a limited degree. A multifaceted approach with shorter work hours as its centrepiece is what is required. Most importantly, it must always be kept in mind that the good health of national economies requires that the appropriate institutional and legislative changes be introduced at a measured pace.

The last word is given to Will Rogers:

Diplomacy is the art of saying 'nice doggie' until you can find a rock.

NOTES

1   O'Riordan, T. (ed.) (1997), *Ecotaxation*, London: Earthscan, p. 3.
2   Honoré, Carl (2004), *In Praise of Slow*, London: Orion.
3   Bunting, Madeleine (2004), *Willing Slaves*, New York: HarperCollins, p. xvii.
4   Even in the midst of life we are all, in some respects, shrouded in what philosopher John Rawls described as a 'veil of ignorance' as to what the future may hold.
5   This analysis assumes that voting outcomes are generally optimal – an assumption that some economists would vigorously dispute. For some background to such dispute see Hardin, Russell (1999), 'Street-level Epistemology and Democratic Participation', paper presented at the meetings of the European Public Choice Society, Lisbon, 7–10 April at http://cniss. wustl.edu/Rikerpapers/hardinpaper1.html, accessed 14 May 2006.
6   See Weil, David N. (2005), *Economic Growth*, Boston: Addison-Wesley, pp. 342–3.
7   The perspicacious reader will appreciate that in the earlier discussion of the fundamental flaw in Chapter 3, it was assumed that taxes are currently at or near the optimal level, meaning that there is currently no inappropriate tax-induced downward bias in work hours that mitigates the effects of the fundamental flaw.
8   Wittman, Donald (1989), 'Why Democracies Produce Efficient Results', *Journal of Political Economy*, **97** (6), 1395–1424.
9   Judt, Tony (2003), 'It's the anti-American way', *Weekend Australian Financial Review*, 17–21 April, Review, p. 11 from *The New York Review of Books*.
10   Henderson, Hazel (1991), *Paradigms in Progress*, San Francisco: Berrett-Koehler, pp. 101 –3.
11   Thus the frequency of animal extinctions per half century, which has increased at an increasing rate since the early 1600s, might have been much lower; see Edwards, S.R. (1995), 'Conserving Biodiversity: Resources for Our Future', Chap. 7 in Bailey, R. (ed.), *The True State of the Planet*, New York: The Free Press.

12 For an introductory discussion of the economics of the assimilative capacity of the economy see Thampapillai, D. (2002), *Environmental Economics*, Melbourne: Oxford University Press, Chap. 2.

13 Of course these monitoring costs are typical defensive expenditures which, although they contribute to GDP, are simply devoted to offsetting the effects of environmental damage. As monitoring costs grow over time they would be a larger and larger proportion of GDP leaving a decreasing proportion of GDP that actually raises well-being.

14 See Messenger, J.C. (2004), *Working Time and Workers' Preferences in Industrialized Countries*, London: Routledge.

15 Material dealing with this policy can be found on the Australian Council of Trade Unions web site at http://www.actu.asn.au/.

16 A little thought reveals that the motivation for these restrictions is often found in negative externalities that the state wishes to limit. It could well be that it is aesthetic considerations rather than prudishness that causes the state to mandate that we cover our bodies.

17 Bunting (2004), p. xx.

18 Putnam, R.D. (2000), *Bowling Alone*, New York: Simon & Schuster, p. 288.

19 Gordon, R.J. (2002), 'Two Centuries of Economic Growth: Europe Chasing the American Frontier', Economic History Workshop, Northwestern University, October, p. 9.

20 de Graff, J., Wann, D. and Naylor, T.D. (2001), *Affluenza*, San Francisco: Berrett-Khoeler, p. 217.

21 Beder, Sharon (2000), *Selling the Work Ethic*, Melbourne: Scribe Publications, p. 248; also see de Graff (2001), pp. 217–8.

22 Cross, Gary (1993), *Time and Money*, London: Routledge, p. 96.

23 See Goklany, I.M. (2002), 'Economic growth and human well-being', Chap. 2. in Morris, Julian (ed.), *Sustainable Development*, London: Profile Books; also see de Graff (2001), p. 219.

24 Putnam (2000), p. 407.

25 I am grateful to James K Boyce who sowed the seeds of this idea by alerting me to the importance that positive externalities can play.

26 In order to simplify this discussion, the important positive externalities that consumption can generate, and that the state could encourage, have been set aside.

8. Intuitive Reasoning versus Deliberative Thought

Most people get their economic beliefs from introspection and their personal experience – the same place that they get their beliefs about most things. Economic theory – and indeed science in general – can serve as an antidote to this kind of introspection.[1]

Hal Varian

The theme of this book has been that if we turn conventional wisdom on its head we can improve work-life balance and our well-being by working less rather than more. Less work means more leisure, less environmental disamenity and a higher quality of life (QOL). It also means less gross domestic product (GDP) per capita; but this is a desirable outcome given that GDP and the well-being of our society are inversely related. This inverse relationship reflects the extreme environmental stress currently imposed on our planet.

This conclusion has been reached by using the mainstream economic paradigm in the context of the wide array of market failures – in particular, negative externalities – that are prominent in the real world.

An important contributor to the current situation characterized by excessive work hours and low QOL is the tendency, discussed in Chapter 3, for society to impute a greater cost to any given level of physical environmental disamenity as GDP per capita increases. This means that even if environmental disamenity were to remain unchanged while GDP per capita increases over time, QOL could not rise at the rate suggested by the rate of increase in GDP per capita. The effect of economic growth on our perception of the costs of environmental damage causes a drag on growth in QOL. Unfortunately, however, the situation is more serious than this. Over time, as GDP per capita has risen, degradation of the environment has actually become worse. Furthermore, research in the area of behavioural economics shows, as we saw in Chapter 5, that the human psyche gives greater weight to losses than to gains. Together, these factors help to explain why, over time, each additional dollar of GDP per capita has caused a decrease rather than an increase in QOL. The net result is falling QOL in the face of rising GDP per capita. Just as an individual can voluntarily, but mistakenly, ruin their health by excessive work effort so a community can do precisely the same thing.

If, to some readers, environmental conditions in developed countries don't seem to be as bad as they have been painted here, it is well to reflect that the transference of environmental damage to offshore havens has significantly reduced the extent of the localized environmental cost borne by middle-class citizens of these developed countries. Furthermore, these middle-class citizens are in a position to expend relatively high levels of income at home to ensure that their living environments are far removed from the heavily trafficked and polluted neighbourhoods that are populated by the less well off. As the Chapter 6 discussion of the relative importance of the fundamental flaw in developed countries as compared to developing countries revealed, if the typical citizen of the developed world was subjected to the full cost of the environmental degradation that they impose on the world environment, the deduction from GDP per capita required to calculate their QOL would be far greater than has been estimated here. The pressing global environmental problems of pollution, loss of species, destruction of habitat, desertification and risk of biological or nuclear destruction are no less real because the high-income earners of the world are able to protect themselves from their immediate effects. Indeed, the rising costs that citizens incur in order to protect themselves from these effects are a manifestation of the capacity of GDP to buy less QOL today than it could 30 years ago.

A recurring theme in the literature that promotes a move to increased leisure time is the idea that the enormous rise in GDP per capita in the US over the past 30 years or so constitutes a productivity dividend that workers have chosen to take in the form of increased incomes rather than increased leisure time. We have shown that this productivity dividend is illusory. Money incomes are higher but QOL is lower and work-life balance is compromised. We are working long hours to produce more output that reduces our well-being. We work these long hours, not because we prefer to take a supposed dividend in the form of higher money incomes, but because two separate factors compel us to do what is not in our best interests.

The first of these factors relates to the fundamental flaw that causes us to work long hours because we compare our work effort to the monetary reward it brings rather than to the much lower environmentally adjusted income (EAI) that takes account of negative externalities and which should be the basis of our decision. The second factor is the desire to work longer hours because the luxury of leisure seems less affordable as our QOL declines. Seen in this light, the tendency for Americans to work long hours by recent historical standards and by comparison with workers in Europe is not paradoxical. This tendency is the natural outcome of a situation where growth in GDP per capita is accompanied by declining QOL. The alarming feature of this finding is that without intervention of some kind, market economies will experience an exponential worsening of the situation: every decline in QOL brings about a tendency to increased work effort, increased GDP and a further decline in QOL. There is no equilibrating factor that will bring about a reversion to an improvement in the situation – except, perhaps, for a doomsday scenario involving a forced decline in economic activity as economies grind to a halt under the burden of pandemic environmental dissipation. We really are on a forced ride to somewhere we do not want to go.

Our economic explanation for the vicious circle of overwork and over consumption sees its root cause as the negative externalities generated by excessive work and production. By contrast, previous critiques of consumerism have been rooted in sociological and psychological explanations of an excessive desire to consume. These critiques do not normally acknowledge that, from society's point of view, the success of any reduction in the desire to consume is dependent on a concomitant decrease in work effort; for if we did consume less but did not work less we would, by definition, save more. This saving provides the wherewithal for investment in newly constructed buildings, plant and equipment.[2] This means that if our work effort remains unchanged, and all the saving that flows from reduced current consumption is used to fund higher levels of investment in capital goods, then current total output of the economy remains unchanged and so does the approximate adverse effect on the environment. The problem, however, is compounded by the fact that a higher level of current investment in capital goods can mean higher future levels of income, higher future levels of consumption and investment, and higher future levels of resource depletion, environmental degradation and congestion. The place to start is not with less consumption but with less work that will guarantee lower consumption and investment – now and in the future.

In his recent book *Collapse*, Jared Diamond devotes a chapter to the question of why some societies make environmentally disastrous decisions. To his list of explanatory factors, which includes failure to anticipate, failure to perceive, rational bad behaviour and disastrous values, we might add 'failure to measure appropriately' – for that is precisely what leads us to produce more measured GDP at the cost of reducing environmental amenity and QOL.[3] The longer we continue to use GDP as a measure of well-being the greater will be the risk of collapse of our own societies as the difference between the rising trend of GDP and the falling trend of QOL widens inexorably.

It was revealed in Chapter 5 that an important dividend from reduced production and consumption will come from a realignment of the relationship between the amount of stuff that we have and the amount of leisure time we have to use it. A reduction in environmental stress accompanying shorter work hours also has the potential to constrain the level of many environmentally malignant activities to within the assimilative capacity of the environment. The pervasive effects of reduced work hours provide a holistic approach to solving our environmental problems – an approach that must, nonetheless, be supported by the piecemeal policies that have thus far characterized modern society's response to an ever worsening situation.

For more than two centuries, calls for lower levels of consumption have come at different times from institutional economists, environmentalists, sociologists and philosophers. By and large, these calls have remained unheeded. As the ecological footprints introduced in Chapter 2 show, the result has been excessive levels of consumption and production in the world as a whole led by the developed world which increasingly sets the erroneous standard by which many developing countries judge their performance.

The explanation for our excessive work effort that is given here involves a classic case of market failure of the type that government policies address on a daily basis. If our tendency to excessive consumption and environmental degradation is seen as a classic case of market failure that sits squarely within the mainstream economic paradigm there is a chance that liberal democratic governments will do something about it. In one sense, they are already doing something about it; they are overseeing piecemeal environmental policies that, by increasing the cost to economic agents of environmentally damaging activities, will, all other factors remaining constant, ultimately reduce production and consumption. Unfortunately, these piecemeal policies are not always able to be implemented, they are slow to act, and they are selective in their application. While implementation of these policies must continue they must be seen as another line of defence which complements, rather than substitutes for, a holistic policy of reduction in work hours.

As was pointed out in Chapter 1, ever since the awakening of environmental concerns in the 1970s, discussion of the extent to which environmental degradation has adversely affected our well-being has been characterized by a debate between optimists and pessimists. Even after more than 30 years of debate to which the best minds of the age have contributed, we are no closer to a consensus. However, the discovery that contemporary economies are characterized by a fundamental flaw that causes us to work and consume and degrade the environment to an extent that is inconsistent with maximization of QOL provides prima facie evidence that the pessimists are correct.

The explanation given here as to why individuals engage in excessive work hours is very different from those given by other critics of the status quo; their explanations variously centre around issues such as the authority of employers who impose work hours on employees, the pervasiveness of advertising and marketing that encourage us to work and consume more by overriding our sovereignty as consumers, and political imperatives that cause national leaders to egg us on to increase GDP in the erroneous (or cynical) belief that it is a valid measure of social progress. Why then has the explanation given here not been given due credence?

The answer may lie in what E.T. Higgins describes as *accessibility* – 'the ease with which particular mental contents come to mind.'[4] Discussing accessibility in his Nobel Prize Lecture, Daniel Kahneman states that intuitive reasoning relies on thoughts that are accessible while deliberative thought processes may be significantly informed by thoughts that are not readily accessible. Nonetheless, it is common for more deliberative thought processes to be misguided by the intuitive thoughts that precede them or lead up to them. Thus if intuition, guided by the accessible information to the effect that firms do a lot of advertising and consumers do a lot of consuming, leads to the idea that over consumption is caused by advertising, this may spawn a vast array of research programmes that use deliberative reasoning to pursue an idea that has intuitive appeal but may have little scientific basis. Similarly, accessible information to the effect that employees have limited short-term choice in respect of work hours, and thus work the hours that their employers expect, may lead to the intuition that workers 'want what they get' in terms of work hours. This may lead to deliberative research designed to support the intuitive hypothesis.

By contrast, the idea that a fundamental flaw in the system hoodwinks workers into working more hours than would maximize their well-being is not intuitive. If it were, it would have surfaced long ago as an explanation for the belief, held by many, that work hours are excessive. No, this is a complex explanation that requires a series of relatively inaccessible deliberative thought processes. Economics, like the physical sciences, has a long history of the overthrow of intuitive ideas by deliberative thought – whether it be Ricardo's idea that a nation that is less efficient at producing all goods may, nonetheless, benefit by trade with a nation that is everywhere more efficient (the theory of comparative advantage), or Keynes's idea that a decision by all citizens to save more may lead to an outcome in which they actually save less (the paradox of thrift). As Kahneman has put it:

Highly accessible features will influence decisions, while features of low accessibility will be largely ignored. Unfortunately, there is no reason to believe that the most accessible features are also the most relevant to a good decision.[5]

NOTES

1   Varian, Hal R. (1996), 'What Use is Economic Theory?', Chap. 20 in Medema, S.G. and Samuels, W.J. (1996), *Foundations of Research in Economics: How Do Economists Do Economics?*, Cheltenham, UK and Brookfield, USA: Edward Elgar, p. 244.
2   From the perspective of Keynesian economics, such a rise in saving might also be associated with high unemployment if appropriate demand management policies were not pursued. The success of governments in avoiding mass unemployment over the past six decades suggests that such a scenario is not likely. Nonetheless, economic growth theory does tell us that excessive saving and subsequent investment can be wasteful of resources.
3   See Diamond, J. (2005), *Collapse*, Camberwell: Allen Lane, Chap. 14.
4   Quoted in Khaneman, Daniel (2002), 'Maps of Bounded Rationality: a Perspective on Intuitive Judgement and Choice', Nobel Prize Lecture, at http://www.nobel.se/economics/laureates /2002/kahnemann-lecture.pdf, p. 4, accessed 25 January 2006.
5   Kahneman, p. 11.

Additional References

Adler, J.H. (2002), 'Do conservation conventions conserve?', Chap. 11 in Morris, J. (ed.), *Sustainable Development,* London: Profile Books.

Anielski, M. (2000), 'Fertile Obfuscation: Making Money Whilst Eroding Living Capital', paper presented at the 34th Annual Conference of the Canadian Economics Association, University of British Columbia, Vancouver, BC, 2–4 June, available at http://members.shaw.ca/ GD2004/ 2004WorkAnielski.htm, p. 6, accessed 30 January 2006.

Ausubel, J.H. (1998), 'Reasons to Worry About the Human Environment', *COSMOS* (Journal of the Cosmos Club in Washington, DC) **8**, 1–12.

Baumol, W.J. and Quandt, R.E. (1964), 'Rules of Thumb and Optimally Imperfect Decisions', *American Economic Review*, **43**, 23–46.

Cairncross, Francis (1992), *Costing the Earth*, Boston, MA: Harvard Business School Press.

Clapp, J (2002), 'Consumption and Environment in a Global Economy', Chap. 7 in Princen, T., Maniates, M. and Conca, K., *Confronting Consumption,* Cambridge, MA: MIT Press, pp. 155–76.

Conca, K. (2002), 'Consumption and Environment in a Global Economy', Chap. 6 in Princen, T., Maniates, M. and Conca, K., *Confronting Consumption,* Cambridge, MA: MIT Press, pp. 133–53.

Del Boca, Daniela (2003), 'Why are fertility and participation rates so low in Italy (and Southern Europe)?', paper prepared for presentation at the Italian Academy at Columbia University, 29 October.

Dhalby, Bev (1998), 'Progressive taxation and the social marginal cost of public funds', *Journal of Public Economics*, **67**, 105–122.

Garnett, Mark (2004), *The Snake that Swallowed Its Tail*, Exeter: Imprint Academic.

Hirst, I.R.C. and Duncan Reekie (eds) (1977), *The Consumer Society,* London: Tavistock Publications.

Honoré, C. (2004), *In Praise of Slow*, London: Orion.

Independent Sector, 'Giving and Volunteering in the United States', available at http://www.independentsector_org/GrandV/s_keyf.htm, accessed 15 May 2006.

Kates, R. W. (2000), 'Population and Consumption: What we know, what we need to know', *Environment*, **42** (3), 10–19.

Lux, K. (2003), 'The failure of the profit motive', *Ecological Economics*, **44**, 1–9.

MacEwan, A. and Weisskopf, T.E. (eds) (1970), *Perspectives on the Economic Problem,* Englewood Cliffs: Prentice Hall.

Manning, Alan (2001), 'Labour supply, search and taxes', *Journal of Public Economics,* **80**, 409–34.

Medema, S.G. and Samuels, W.J. (eds) (1996), *Foundations of Research in Economics: How Do Economists Do Economics?*, Cheltenham, UK and Brookfield, USA: Edward Elgar.

Pocock, Barbara (2003), *The Work/Life Collision*, Sydney: Federation Press.

Sagoff, Mark (1988), *The Economy of the Earth*, Cambridge: Cambridge University Press.

Sillamaa, M.A. (1999), Comment 'Taxpayer behaviour in response to taxation: comment and new experimental evidence', *Journal of Accounting and Public Policy*, **18**, 165–77.

Smith, Adam (1869), *An Enquiry into the Nature and Causes of the Wealth of Nations*, Rogers, J.E.T. (ed.), Oxford: Oxford University Press.

Sørensen, P.B. (1999), 'Optimal tax progressivity in imperfect labour markets', *Labour Economics*, **6**, 435–52.

Stiglitz, J.E. (2002), 'New perspectives on public finance: recent achievements and future challenges', *Journal of Public Economics*, **86**, 341–60.

Stockhausen, Gerard (1998), 'Leisure in the economic thought of John Paul II', *International Journal of Social Economics*, **25** (11/12), 1672–83.

Stopher, P. R. (2004), 'Reducing road congestion: a reality check', *Transport Policy*, **11** (2), 117–31.

Templet, P.H. (1995), 'Grazing the Commons: an empirical analysis of externalities, subsidies and sustainability', *Ecological Economics*, **12**, 141–59.

Williams-Ellis, C. (ed.) (1938), *Britian and the Beast*, London: Readers' Union.

York, R., Rosa, E.A. and Dietz, T. (2003), 'STIRPAT, IPAT and ImPACT: analytic tools for unpacking the driving forces of environmental impacts', *Ecological Economics,* **46**, 351–65.

Index